JANE CAMPION

PHILOSOPHICAL FILMMAKERS

Series editor: Costica Bradatan is a Professor of Humanities at Texas Tech University, USA, and an Honorary Research Professor of Philosophy at the University of Queensland, Australia. He is the author of *Dying for Ideas: The Dangerous Lives of the Philosophers* (Bloomsbury, 2015), among other books.

Films can ask big questions about human existence: what it means to be alive, to be afraid, to be moral, to be loved. The *Philosophical Filmmakers* series examines the work of influential directors, through the writing of thinkers wanting to grapple with the rocky territory where film and philosophy touch borders.

Each book involves a philosopher engaging with an individual filmmaker's work, revealing how it has inspired the author's own philosophical perspectives and how critical engagement with those films can expand our intellectual horizons.

Other titles in the series:

Eric Rohmer, Vittorio Hösle

Werner Herzog, Richard Eldridge

Terrence Malick, Robert Sinnerbrink

Kenneth Lonergan, Todd May

Shyam Benegal, Samir Chopra

Douglas Sirk, Robert B. Pippin

Lucasfilm, Cyrus R. K. Patell

Christopher Nolan, Robbie B. H. Goh

Alfred Hitchcock, Mark William Roche

Luchino Visconti, Joan Ramon Resina

Theo Angelopoulos, Vrasidas Karalis

Alejandro Jodorowsky, William Egginton

István Szabó, Susan Rubin Suleiman

Other titles forthcoming:

Leni Riefenstahl, Jakob Lothe

Bong Joon Ho, Anthony Curtis Adler

JANE CAMPION

Filmmaker and Philosopher

BERNADETTE WEGENSTEIN

BLOOMSBURY ACADEMIC
LONDON • NEW YORK • OXFORD • NEW DELHI • SYDNEY

BLOOMSBURY ACADEMIC
Bloomsbury Publishing Plc
50 Bedford Square, London, WC1B 3DP, UK
1385 Broadway, New York, NY 10018, USA
29 Earlsfort Terrace, Dublin 2, Ireland

BLOOMSBURY, BLOOMSBURY ACADEMIC and the Diana logo are trademarks of Bloomsbury Publishing Plc

First published in Great Britain 2025

Cover image: *The Power of the Dog* (2021 UK)
Directed by Jane Campion. Shown: Kodi Smit-McPhee
Netflix/Photofest © Netflix

A catalogue record for this book is available from the British Library.

A catalog record for this book is available from the Library of Congress.

ISBN: HB: 978-1-3501-6206-8
PB: 978-1-3501-6207-5
ePDF: 978-1-3501-6208-2
eBook: 978-1-3501-6209-9

Series: Philosophical Filmmakers

Typeset by Deanta Global Publishing Services, Chennai, India
Printed and bound in Great Britain

To find out more about our authors and books visit www.bloomsbury.com and sign up for our newsletters.

CONTENTS

FIGURES

1

Is Campion a "Feminist Filmmaker" and Has This Question Become Obsolete?

> I prefer to think of films as meditations, a beautiful meditation that your mind naturally comes back to because it trusts the material.
>
> JANE CAMPION, 2005 (Deb Verhoeven, Jane Campion, 184)

The opportunity to write about filmmaker Jane Campion's feminism would be a pleasure to a feminist and film theorist under any circumstances but, after 2022, such a prompt is truly a gift, for her victory at the Oscars as one of only three women directors, after Kathryn Bigelow and Chloé Zhao, to win an Academy Award for Best Director affords a retroactive clarity to those looking for feminist and philosophical carry-throughs in her cinematic corpus. I can say as a media scholar as well as a documentary filmmaker, one as committed as Campion to putting women's stories on the screen, that the chance to write about her now is almost too good to be true. I have watched Campion's films throughout my entire life, in what I could divide into three phases: when I was in my twenties and simply loving films like *The Piano* without yet understanding exactly why or even yet thinking of her as a feminist putting women's stories on the screen; then when I was conducting academic research as a film and media scholar on her work from France, Italy, and the United States between the 1990s and 2000s; and finally now, when I am making my own films and taking inspiration from her. The joy of seeing Campion's feminism now become mainstream seems to dovetail with my own journey through her oeuvre.

Campion and her filmic work can first be positioned in the context of "women directors" in "world cinema," in a sector that Rosalind Galt and Karl Schoonover have called "global art cinema."[1] In this ecosystem, sustained by highly selective and mostly European film festivals and "specialty exhibition" events that together cultivate prestige around the figure of the auteur, "[w]omen directors are better represented [. . .] than in the U.S. commercial sector."[2] Initiatives at international film festivals—for instance, the Hubert Bals Fund from the Rotterdam Film Festival, the World Cinema Fund from the Berlinale, Women at Sundance, and various funding initiatives from the Athena Film Festival to the Geena Davis Institute on Gender in Media—have invested in women's cinema through "world cinema" funds for over a decade now. In her pivotal *Women's Cinema, World Cinema*, Patricia White remembers the 2007 anniversary project from the Cannes Film Festival, *Chacun son cinéma/To Each His Own*

Cinema, which does not import the default Romance masculine pronoun "chacun" by coincidence, as is confirmed by the English title.[3] Rather, it crystallizes the problem of women's filmmaking and Campion's unique position with it. The Cannes *Chacun son cinéma* website announces that "35 directors, from 5 different continents and 25 countries, all universally recognised, pay tribute, in 3 minutes each, to the motion picture theater, that magical venue of communion par excellence of film lovers the world over."[4] What is not being said is that Campion was the only woman included. As White poignantly analyzes in her chapter "To Each *Her* Own Cinema," at Cannes, "Campion is made to embody Woman, the sole femme—not one woman (director) among many."[5] Cannes appointed Campion head of a majority-female jury that year but, in her public speech, she refused to sweep the problem under the rug:

> there's some inherent sexism in the industry. Thierry Frémaux told us that only 7% of the [. . .] 1,800 films that were submitted to the Cannes Film Festival were directed by women. And he was proud to say, "Well, actually we have 20% in all the different programs." But, nevertheless, it does feel very undemocratic and women do notice, you know. Time and time again, we don't get our share of representation. You know, excuse me, gentlemen, but, you know, the guys do seem to eat all the cake, so to speak. And it's not that I resent the male filmmakers—I love all of them—but there is something that women are thinking of doing that we don't get to know enough about. And it's always a surprise for the world when a woman filmmaker does come about and you get a more feminine vision.[6]

As some continue to point out, Campion did not want to be identified as a feminist in the cookie-cutter model of contemporary partisan conformity: "Her feminism, she says, should speak for itself, but she resists anything that smacks of feminist pieties or of unfriendliness to men."[7] Some theorists have argued—and I would follow this line of argumentation—that the feminist label fails to fully capture the dilemmas of Campion's characters, who are mainly cisgender girls and women searching for heteronormative love or working through their dysfunctional family situations. But as I will demonstrate and discuss in this book, I believe that Campion's feminism is performed and inspired by a profound activism, not one that simply ends at her characters' quests. What is central—besides the stories she adapts and brings to the screen, predominantly stories of struggling women—is her commitment to *women making movies*, a strong claim for gender equality in the film industry.[8] In 1993, the year she won the Palme d'Or for *The Piano*, Campion herself spoke to the *New York Times* about the Australian collective Women's Film Unit, in which she participated early in her career:

> Basically, the way film sets work is very undemocratic, whereas the idea behind the unit—the idealism—predisposed its members to expect a lot more say. On a normal set, the priority is the work; in a situation like the Women's Film Unit, the politics were the work. All the same, the unit did address a major inequality. Also, there was a radical feminist group, filmmakers and activists, who had a huge impact on the Australian Film Commission. They were astonishing in their ability to intimidate the bureaucracy into supporting more women. But I think it's quite clear in my work

> that my orientation isn't political or doesn't come out of modern politics.[9]

Sue Thornham also describes Campion as "refusing post-feminism's easy resolutions."[10] But I believe that tiptoeing around Campion when tracing a feminist film history would be a mistake.

As Alison Butler points out in *Women's Cinema: The Contested Screen*, the understanding of authorship itself does not really apply in the same way to women's cinema and men's: "for female filmmakers, for whom the act of authoring is already complicated by social conditions and cultural conventions, authorship is not so much a question of deconstruction as one of *re*construction. Insistence on the authoring presence of the woman outside the text is a formal and tactical necessity."[11] White also observes that nontheatrical, experimental, documentary, and collaborative work does not "line up easily within traditional auteurist discourses of genius and ownership."[12] Geetha Ramanathan's very helpful *Feminist Auteurs: Reading Women's Films* closely analyzes the visual, sonic, and narrative divergences from the male-auteur model through which feminist filmmakers have established their own authority.[13] Ramanathan also identifies limitations that women filmmakers have overcome to portray their own desires and avoiding the trap of their "to-be-looked-at-ness," as Laura Mulvey described the position of women under the male gaze.[14]

From the point of view of feminist philosophy, Campion's resistance to the category of feminist filmmaking corresponds to the "othering" of women's films, seen as differences from a male standard, including holding them to a different value system. When the rules of the system define women *against* men, not the other way around, the women remain stuck in the same conundrum Luce Irigaray articulated about patriarchal societies in general.[15] Rick Altman and many other critics have pointed to the paradox that women's films are defined by a notion of "gendered address," that is, by the gender of their most receptive audience.[16] To include a recent anecdote from my own filmmaking, I very consciously titled my 2021 documentary *The Conductor* with a gender-neutral term in order to play with the audience's expectation that it would likely be about a male conductor and make viewers self-aware of their own bias when this film actually tells the life story of a woman conductor, Marin Alsop. In other words, women's film, understood in this way, is a genre defined by viewers and viewing practices, not by a point of view or the identity of the filmmaker. In this context, Jami Bernard's catalog *Chick Flicks: A Movie Lover's Guide to the Movies Women Love* places *The Piano* in the category of "Emotional Rescue" among films that will satisfy a female audience.[17]

White's analysis of global women's cinema, in fact, looks at how "elite definitions of art cinema and auteurism attempt to brand the careers of particular women directors. These rare cineastes in turn deploy their privileged status to bring to light connections and affinities that dominant discourses of auteurism would overlook, such as the relationship between artist and female image or between the female body and the nation."[18] To say it with bell hooks:

> *The Piano* seduces and excites audiences with its uncritical portrayal of sexism and misogyny. Reviewers and audiences alike seem to assume that Campion's gender, as well as her breaking of traditional boundaries that inhibit the advancement of women in film, indicate that her work expresses a feminist standpoint. And

> indeed she does employ feminist tropes even as her work betrays feminist visions of female actualization, celebrating and eroticizing male domination.[19]

I will return to this fascinating distinction between "feminism" and "chick flicks" in a close reading of *The Piano* in my third chapter, and in Chapter 4 with a critical discussion of the thriller genre, which Campion turns to with *In the Cut*, another film for which she was equally accused of not being feminist enough.

So, what are Campion's own gender politics? *The Lady Bug*, her three-minute contribution to *Chacun son cinéma* in 2007, says it all. An experimental "homage to her favorite filmmaker, [Luís] Buñuel" that Campion also described as "a sort of feminist thing," the short offers a satirical commentary on women's chances in the world.[20] In the opening sequence, the little hybrid and partly animated ladybug, voiced by co-writer Erica Englert, says tellingly: "I am here for one reason only: to find out who I am. [. . .] It is not as easy as it sounds for a lady to find out who she is." A janitor, cleaning up what looks like a classroom, hears the ladybug's voice behind the screen of a loudspeaker and seems to grow annoyed by her. The ladybug is having a conversation with a male counterpart, voiced by Clayton Jacobson, whom we never see but who reacts cynically to the ladybug's "whining about the lack of opportunity." The janitor, made to articulate a metaphor for male power and shown with big shoes that overpower the ladybug's body size by at least four times, is so irritated listening to her complaints that he tries to stomp her to death: "If you don't shut up, I am going to squash you." But she gets away. (Figures 1 and 2)

FIGURES 1 AND 2 *Stills from* The Lady Bug, *2007.*

Though on occasion Campion has been, as White remembers, "cagey about the use of the word 'feminist' to describe herself, she certainly acknowledges feminist themes in her work and the centrality of women's desire to it."[21] I would add that the surrealist ladybug speaks for the director herself: "It is not so easy for a ladybug to find out who she is." In a 1984 interview with Mark Stiles, Campion tells the story of how she herself found out who she really was, just like the ladybug:

> I am also a girl and I thought that if very clever, ambitious boys do this stuff, then why shouldn't girls? It sounds corny, but I really did think like that. [. . .] When all my boyfriends ran out [there] was nobody and I was by myself [and] I realized I could no longer attach myself to someone else and be just that: an attachment. So I said, "Okay, I'll have to go myself." And I suddenly felt this incredible new interest in life and this great excitement.[22]

As a woman invited to present her films alone among other male directors in top-tier film events like Cannes and the Oscars, Campion has, in fact, been very outspoken about her political feelings and ideas about being "the only woman" in the field. One could even go as far as to identify her as a feminist activist during these public

FIGURE 3 *Cannes Film Festival, Jane Campion in a sea of male directors.*

performances. Much like other women pioneers, Campion recounts that, at the age of twenty-five, she made the decision to expose herself completely and fail if necessary.[23] Interestingly, Alsop, the first woman to break the glass ceiling in the male-dominated field of classical music conducting, exhibited similar wisdom in my abovementioned documentary, *The Conductor*: "You have to be able to fail massively, and completely, because otherwise you will only ever play it safe."[24] Campion's recipe for success is similar. It is not only launching oneself into a possible failure and rejection but, as she says, it is also a combination of inspiration and fear: "You just need one degree more inspiration than fear."[25]

After a short introduction quoting one of her films, Julie Bertuccelli's recent documentary *Jane Campion: la femme cinéma* (*Jane Campion: The Cinema Woman*) opens with a question posed to Campion at the 1993 Cannes Film Festival, in an ocean of thirty-five men (Figure 3), as the only one woman to present a film as director that year.

Here, before anyone knew she would win the Palme d'Or that year, a French journalist asked her, "How do you feel being the only woman among all these men in this selection, which is a bit macho [*machist*] maybe?" While some of the men look away and others look at the director with an air of guilt, Campion responds, "I think it's really a reflection of how things really are right now." She pauses and adds, "Sadly."[26] After some embarrassed laughter and the follow-up question from the journalist, asking whether she meant in cinema or elsewhere, Campion specifies, "Probably everywhere."[27] The on-site camera now frames Campion in close-up, revealing two male directors behind her, seeming slightly disturbed and nervous, as she continues about what the feminine is for her as director: "I think the feminine is such a strong and important aspect to our humanity. I think we are goddesses, we are beautiful, we're intuitive, we're nurturing. So much of the media or the way we see the world is written and thought of by men that really don't know what women think."[28] Campion vows that with her films she is making a commitment to what women have to say, especially regarding power: "Women have no power in the real world. But women have secrets, and secrets are empowering."[29]

It is an apt opening to a professional biography marked by the difficulties of a woman growing into the male-dominated industry of filmmaking. As she told the *National Times* in 1985, "It's harder being a woman director because on the whole women don't have husbands or boyfriends who are willing to be like wives."[30] But Campion supported herself in part by fostering the company of other women pioneering in the industry: for example, Sally Bongers, the camera operator for her breakthrough short *Peel*, was the first woman in Australia to shoot a 35-mm film. For *Sweetie*, many other crewmembers were also women and it was reported that men on the crew mistreated these women, including Campion herself, who remembers the camera assistant making her feel that she had no idea how to make a film. Experiences such as these made an impact on Campion's collaborative decisions: the editor of her early films from *Passionless Moments* to *An Angel at My Table*, Veronika Jenet, observes that "Jane always surrounds herself with people who are very supportive and give her free range."[31] Having read a woman's circumstances in the industry into the medium itself, Campion has identified "a different kind of vulnerability when a woman is directing," as she told Marli Feldvoss in an interview for the German journal *EPD Film*.[32] But when a woman does direct, how does the industry in turn receive her work?

In the 2019 Governor's Award speech by directors Jane Campion and Greta Gerwig, who had been nominated for her directorial debut film *Lady Bird* (2017), celebrating the Governor's Award bestowed on Italian feminist filmmaker Lina Wertmüller, Campion tells the history of women considered for the Academy Award for Best Director, which she calls poignantly "a very short history, more of a haiku": "First there was Lina, four more are nominated, then Katherine won. So the number of nominations for women—" at which point Campion, whose nomination in 1993 for *The Piano* made her one of the four nominees she just mentioned, interrupts her story and holds up one hand with her five fingers spread out.[33] The audience laughs at the performance of the visual citation and, after Campion shows five women on one hand, she then flashes the ten fingers of both her hands thirty-five times to arrive at the total of 350 nominations and seventy awards for male directors. Campion points out in an afterthought that the distribution is "staggeringly unequal."[34]

To top this accounting, she goes on to state that the first and last time a woman ever experiences equality is after being born, when the baby is examined and called "a girl" or "a boy."[35] After that, equality for women descends, as she recounts with a cynical smile. "How do you correct centuries of patriarchal domination?" she asks before introducing Wertmüller and her 1975 film *Pasqualino Settebellezze*, which she not only admires personally but which was the first film by a woman director to be nominated for an Oscar for Best Director (as well as for Best Foreign Film and Best Picture).[36] Is Campion a feminist and even an outspoken one? I would reply, after this public address and performance, how can there be any doubt about it? Two years after this provocative Oscar speech by Campion and Gerwig, two women have since won an Oscar for Best Director. In 2021, Zhao wins for *Nomadland* and in 2022, Campion herself wins for her latest film, *The Power of the Dog*, for which she is also awarded the Prix Lumière at the Lumière Film Festival, the Silver Lion at the Venice International Film Festival, and many others. The media and even Campion herself suddenly stop tiptoeing around the question of whether Campion is or was a feminist. I will return to the way Jane Campion has influenced and perhaps changed what a "female auteur means" after Greta Gerwig directed the Hollywood hit *Barbie* in 2023, in the book's Conclusion, when Greta Gerwig, Noah Baumbach, and Jane Campion talk through writing and directing *Barbie* on Zoom.

Before I discuss the films and Campion's style in detail, I want to point out a few biographical references about her that were of particular interest to me researching and writing this book. Campion was born and raised in Wellington, New Zealand, but both of her parents were trained as stage actors in England and became "prominent figures in New Zealand theatre," and her father Richard was even considered a "giant of New Zealand theatre."[37] Daughters Anna, two years her senior, and Jane grew up in an environment of theater, film, and culture. Shakespeare was a household name for the Campions and was treated like the Bible. Her relationship to New Zealand stayed very positive, throughout her career, even though she moved to study, and eventually live and work in Australia. Campion studied anthropology and art as an undergraduate in New Zealand, and then moved to Australia. But New Zealand remains a point of reference for Campion all throughout her life, including in terms of her feminist awareness. She proudly mentioned in various interviews that New Zealand became the first self-governing nation in the world where women won the right to vote in 1893. In an interview with New Zealand's *Mail & Guardian* that she gave after *The Portrait of a Lady* came out in 1996, Campion even declares that the location of New Zealand, a tiny country at the edge of the world, informed her *way of seeing*.

> a country where personal matters are kept personal, a country founded on a Utopian ideal of equality that ended up flattening out difference. Campion talks of the uncelebratory nature of New Zealand. You know, she says, "they used to have a programme on TV in New Zealand called That's Fairly Interesting. That's the title of it. In America, it's That's Incredible! New Zealand is really a country of enormous understatement."[38]

Two other aspects of Campion's youth stand out. One is the story she has told several times about passing an unexpectedly cold winter in Italy and becoming terribly depressed. What was supposed to be a beautiful experience became the source of suffering, a motive I find in several of Campion's heroines. In *The Portrait of a Lady*, for instance, Isabel's desired love, her passion, and her fantasies turn into her biggest nightmares. As Alistair Fox points out in his psychoanalytic reading of Campion's films up until 2009, it is most likely that Campion's own unhappy travels mirrored themselves in her account of Isabel Archer's experience traveling back to Europe, her roots, in *The Portrait of a Lady* (see Chapter 3).[39] A second relevant moment from her biography is that, as Campion remembers her time as a student at the Sydney College of the Arts, she was mostly thinking about relationships but, when she started making "story paintings," she suddenly realized "she was trying to tell stories."[40] These stories, as she tells in interviews, seem to have come out of her as lived experiences: "I decided I wanted to do work about things I was thinking about and involved in, which were generally relationships and love . . . and sex!"[41] The stories did not only talk about female desire, sex, and love, but they presented a new point of view in the auteur film: a woman's world.

Campion, the Once Rare Case of a Female Auteur

We all know that Campion is a woman director, one of the six women to be nominated for Best Director and one of three to win. But we also know the Oscars are not the most serious standard of filmmaking, as they are also a political entity that reacts to public pressure. Is it a coincidence that Zhao won an Oscar immediately after Campion delivered her criticism of the scarcity of women in the industry?

We cannot know but, what is more, we need not. What matters is that the profile of women filmmakers was raised by Campion both speaking up and making herself known for her own authorship and for becoming an auteur. But what is an auteur?

For Ryan Uytdewilligen, an auteur is "an artist who applies a high amount of stylistic control over their craft. In the case of Auteur Filmmaking, this would be the director."[42] I would add that an auteur is also a filmmaker whose style is recognizable, allowing us to visually identify a "Hitchcock film" or a "Buñuel film." An auteur is someone who turns every story, whether it is written by them, or adapted from an existing piece of literature, into *their* story. To accomplish the consistency of their authorship, an auteur also often works with the same actors, as they inhabit the auteur's point of view and have moved in with them, so to speak. For instance, the Australian actor Geneviève Lemon has been featured prominently in Campion's work from *Sweetie* and *The Piano* to the *Top of the Lake* television series (2013–17) and *The Power of the Dog* and was also part of "the voices" in *The Lady Bug*. The Californian actress Elisabeth Moss, for her part, became a classic "Campion actor" during the production of both seasons of *Top of the Lake* and, most recently, Kirsten Dunst has joined the club that also includes Rose Gordon. It is no coincidence that I reference the full body of a director's work when thinking of them as an "auteur." In fact, the term "auteur" dates to 1962, when the US critic Andrew Sarris published an essay in which he describes the circle around the French journal *Cahiers du cinéma*, spearheaded by André Bazin, and proposes that auteur theory evaluates the body of a director's work rather than its isolated masterpieces. In this framework, special attention is given to "true form" and the resulting interpretation positions the director in conversation with "his own previous work," since the auteurs mentioned by Sarris are, unsurprisingly, only men, and they have, to say it with Kaja Silverman, the "heroic proportion of the romantic author":[43]

> Two recent films—*Boccaccio '70* and *The Seven Capital Sins*—unwittingly reinforced the *auteur* theory by confirming the relative standing of the many directors involved. If I had not seen either film, I would have anticipated that the order of merit in *Boccaccio '70* would be [Luchino] Visconti, [Federico] Fellini, and [Vittorio] De Sica, and in *The Seven Capital Sins* [Jean-Luc] Godard, [Claude] Chabrol, [Jacques] Demy, [Roger] Vadim, [Philippe] De Broca, [Édouard] Molinaro. [. . .] However, [. . .] even in these frothy, ultracommercial servings of entertainment, the contribution of each director had less in common stylistically with the work of other directors on the project than with his own previous work.[44]

With *The Power of the Dog* from 2021, Campion was officially initiated into the old boys' club of auteurs. Accordingly, the reception of *The Power of the Dog* by the media was at times more concerned more with the filmmaker than the film, which adheres to the typical reception of an auteur's film. However, the form of this most recent film did not relate to Campion's earlier work in terms of genre. In her recent article, "Women Auteurs, Western Promises," White advances *The Power of the Dog* as an auteur film, not only in thematic motifs and stylistic signature but also in its production and reception.[45] In fact, in her portrait of Campion, Jordan Kisner describes Campion as "the most decorated female filmmaker alive, an auteur in the lineage of Luis Buñuel, François Truffaut, and Pedro Almodóvar."[46] But *The*

Power of the Dog is not a film that lets us see the world through a female character's eyes in the way Campion's earlier work had because such a perspective is no longer the primary necessity. In various interviews and public appearances, Campion stated that with this film, she felt she could allow herself to tell different stories, with men as the lead characters: "I felt I can make a film with a male lead now as there are more women directors creating stories with female leads."[47] It is certainly noteworthy that Campion wins an Oscar for a film in what could not be a more historically masculine genre, the Western, which has traditionally celebrated heroic male domination, the North American and—in the context of the Spaghetti Western—Italian appropriation of the host culture and then the owning and sharing of the foreign "open" territories through cinema. Furthermore, there has always been an internationalism written into the Western genre that befits the global recognition of *The Power of the Dog* and its international production. In the case of *The Power of the Dog*, this internationalism is driven by British actor Benedict Cumberbatch's portrayal of the main character Phil Burbank.

Linking Campion to the Argentine auteur Lucrecia Martel and the Iranian Samira Makhmalbaf, White argues that "these talented directors reflect on their own position by problematizing the figure of the exceptional woman in their work."[48] With Martel, Campion shares much of her love of awkwardness and the interest in young women's bodies, particularly school uniforms and the bare feet and knees underneath them, evident in Martel's 2004 *La niña santa* (*The Holy Girl*) among others. The figure of the exceptional girl or woman is not only at the core of Campion's oeuvre until *The Power of the Dog* but also comes at the expense of the male characters that do not enjoy the same depth of development, if any. In fact, Bertuccelli's recent documentary shows several interviews with Campion, in which she states very clearly that, in her early years of filmmaking, she wanted to tell stories not told by "the boys," a.k.a. male directors in the mainstream business, but, rather, stories about women outsiders and freaks or, as she herself calls them, "willful weird women."[49] Such women populate films throughout Campion's career: first is Dawn, a delusional young woman with the eponymous nickname in *Sweetie*, and then the delusional cult member Ruth in *Holy Smoke!* In *The Piano*, one of Campion's historical films, we are quite literally in the mind of mute Ada McGrath, a mid-nineteenth-century Scottish pianist who has arrived in New Zealand with her young daughter and her piano. There is also Isabel Archer, played by the then relatively undiscovered Australian actor Nicole Kidman in Campion's adaptation of *The Portrait of a Lady*, who has lustful fantasies of group sex, not made explicit in Henry James's novel which the film is based on. And there is also the red-headed Janet Frame in *An Angel at My Table*, based on Frame's autobiography, which recounts struggling with mental illness and growing up in an impoverished family in New Zealand. And not to forget the sad and seemingly autistic character of Robin Griffin in *Top of the Lake*—played by Moss, another Australian—a willfully weird detective who returns to her native New Zealand after living in Australia for many years to solve the disappearance of a twelve-year-old girl.

The risk that Campion takes as a storyteller is telling stories and exposing unusual themes around her "willful weird women" that audiences have not seen before. To put this in terms of a classic mythological analysis of Campion's heroines, I would like to consider Maria Tatar's *The Heroine with 1001 Faces*, a rewriting of and response to Joseph Campbell's 1949 *The Hero with a Thousand Faces*, which had not considered the journey of female heroines in its classic analysis of the archetypal and exclusively male "hero's" mythical journey.[50] To understand Campion's willful women, it is not enough to look at what they *do or say aloud* but also what they *don't do* or perhaps only what they *think*. To do justice to a feminist heroine, it is thus insufficient to compare them to male heroes in the classic format of the myth, but, as Tatar suggests, we must consider other genres, such as fairy tales or old wives' tales, where women are indeed speaking out and telling stories themselves. To relate this relationship with genre to the unique heroism of women in the realm of film, I want to stress that by looking at Campion's heroines' journeys in detail, we can detect a different syntax of the heroine than in conventional male auteurs' hero's journeys.

Through her films, Campion talks about people who live in difficult circumstances and, in particular, about how women, who often live in such difficult circumstances, *feel*. As she tells the *Cahiers du cinéma* in 1993, after her breakthrough receiving the Palme d'Or for *The Piano*, "There are not a lot of films where the heroes are women."[51] Not only are Campion's heroes women, and her films—with the exception of *The Power of the Dog*—stories about women but, more importantly, Campion's women have sexual drives and fantasies that range from exploring their own genitals or putting on lipstick for the first time, as with her earlier shorts, to a sexual obsession with a male police chief trying to solve a series of crimes committed by a serial killer, as with Frannie Avery played by Meg Ryan in the 2003 feature *In the Cut*, or an obsession with solving crimes against women in the case of the disappearance of a twelve-year-old girl in a remote community in New Zealand, as with Moss's character Detective Griffin in *Top of the Lake*. Starting with one of her very first short films, *A Girl's Own Story* from 1984, female sexuality has been at the center of Campion's cinematic investigations. In my second chapter, I will dive deeply into Alistair Fox's reading of not only Campion's characters' sexuality but also their fantasy structure, in Fox's at times patronizing and even disturbing analysis of Campion's own sexual drive behind her films.[52] In her own words, Campion reports that, throughout her formative youthful years, sexuality was what she was writing about for many years, and especially the struggle of finding a sexual self during her formative years: "I was absorbed with so many issues of being a woman."[53] Campion says that what really interests her about sexuality, in fact, is that it is a "mind thing."[54] The sexual "mind thing" is definitely active in her latest work, the film that initiated Campion into the knighthood of the auteur. In *The Power of the Dog*, Phil Burbank is struggling with his hidden homosexuality that drives the entire internal narrative and external visual structure of the film, which I will discuss in detail in my fourth chapter. In addition to inquiring into sexuality, my investigation of the film will be about the Western genre itself and the way in which Campion rewrote this genre into her own feminist auteurial signature.

Campion as a Philosophical Filmmaker

In addition to safely labeling Campion a "female auteur," how can we describe the stylistic control she holds over her films, such that we recognize them as "Campion films"? Put differently, to what extent are her themes philosophically universal? As Randall Halle states, "the interrelationship of film and philosophy as a direction in film studies has enjoyed a growth of research."[55] The central question, then, is what philosophy can reveal to see the meaning of a film more clearly. For Halle, the main influences for the philosophy of film are the works on film by Gilles Deleuze, as well as some of the phenomenologists who were central to Deleuze including Jean Epstein, Maurice Merleau-Ponty and Edmund Husserl.[56] In this sense, the philosophy of film understands film *as* philosophy.[57] In the eleven principles of "creating visual alterity" that Halle lists, I will honor a few that have been a driving force for my own approach to analyzing Campion's oeuvre: "Seeing of something is always from a particular perspective in place and time"; "Seeing is dynamic"; "the apparatus of sight must be understood as a differentiating apparatus capable of ever increasing distinction"; "we can refer to this unfolding dynamic process of preconscious differentiation as visual alterity."[58] I will start by listing some thematic threads and narratives that weave themselves throughout Campion's work to ask how such a "visual alterity" is created in her films. The first is women's sexuality, especially a young woman's sexuality, prominent in her earlier films. Another concern is belief and its deconstruction. Another complex of themes is the interaction between nature, memory, and the power of secrets, with which films like *Holy Smoke!* or *The Power of the Dog* create a different kind of ontological belief system that leaves behind realism for a metaphysics of the place and its surrounding nature. Each of these considerations will be discussed at length throughout the following chapters, but for now, they can be usefully situated in a chronology of Campion's early work.

In this introductory context, I would also like to briefly survey the themes surrounding women's sexuality and the precarity of the family system in Campion's earliest shorts and features. Campion's very first film, the 1980 *Tissues*, is a brilliant short that got her accepted into the Australian School of Film and Television. While I won't be including this film in my analysis in Chapter 2, I want to allude to some important themes in it. Already in *Tissues*, Campion shows some of the main concerns and images that will substantiate many of her later films: a dysfunctional family life, in particular a difficult and abusive mother-daughter relationship exacerbated by the mother's depression; young girls in school uniforms; some form of on-screen nudity or sex; and a surrealist plot, which here resembles both *The Lady Bug* and the 1983 short *Passionless Moments*, a sequence of wry satirical experimental vignettes about daily life drawn from awkward moments and absurdist storylines. In this earlier short—which she wrote with her then partner, Gerard Lee—Campion probes characters who seem lost and in search of something. In one "koan," a voice-over narrator tells the story of a little boy who is convinced the beans he has just bought will explode in twenty seconds.[59] We see the boy approach the camera and then run away as fast as he can, but the story finds no real narrative solution. While these films are very noteworthy, I won't be discussing them in more detail in Chapter 2, the Transgressive Gaze, as they don't fully represent the kind of transgressions, particularly of sexual nature, that I want to discuss.

Another short, the 1984 film *After Hours*, which I will include in Chapter 2, did indeed deal with the topic of sexuality, and specifically sexual abuse and violation at the workplace. The film won the IXL award at the Melbourne Film Festival, but Campion admits she did not enjoy making it as it was just a "normal film" and its feminism felt not natural but, rather, commissioned and therefore contrived:

> I don't like *After Hours* a lot because I feel like the reasons for making it were impure. I felt a conflict between the project and my artistic conscience. The film [due to its funding] had to be openly feminist since it spoke about the sexual abuse of women at work. I wasn't comfortable because I don't like films that say how one should or shouldn't behave. I think that the world is more complicated than that. I prefer watching people, studying their behavior without blaming them. I would have preferred to have put this film in a closet.[60]

While Campion did not feel this was "her" film, as it was produced and commissioned by the Women's Film Unit of Film Australia and clearly, as she felt that the producers "cornered her" into the model of a particular "feminist filmmaker," the film is nonetheless interesting, for it exposes a situation that could not be more topical today: consent and sexuality in the workplace. I will return to a in-depth discussion of this film in Chapter 2.

Particularly noteworthy is her 1982 short *Peel*, which in fact placed her on the international horizon of up-and-coming filmmakers. The film was inspired by the family of Australian fashion designer Katie Pye, all of whom played themselves in the production. The film presents a family crisis during a car ride, when the father pulls over on the highway after losing patience with his two children teasing each other. The father's ultimate loss of control stems from the son peeling an orange, which drives the entire family crazy. All members of the family are neurotic and, to a certain degree, unsympathetic characters but there is a secret about them and an unspoken interdependency that binds them to each other. While making *Peel*, Campion learned that she had to "take everything away to be able to see": on a meta-cinematic level, we could say that the job of cinema here was to "peel" away the skin of the characters and experiences to expose their real selves or a deeper truth that only exists in the realm of cinema itself.[61] Again, I will include Alistair Fox's reading of the orange as an expression of a repressed sexuality in my second chapter. *Peel* also taught Campion the physical risks posed by exhausting filmmaking, when she was hospitalized by the end of production in what she recounts as a warning sign for her future filmmaking. For instance, when *The Piano* came out in 1993, Campion was pregnant with her first child, a son called Jasper. She had to leave the festival where she would receive the Cannes Palme d'Or to deliver the baby. But Jasper only lived for twelve days and, as Campion recalls, the year she received the highest prize in her career thus far, she also suffered her deepest personal loss.

Campion had become internationally noticed as a filmmaker when she was thirty-two, after *Peel* won the Golden Palm for Best Short Film at Cannes in 1986. In many interviews, Campion recounts getting the unexpected call that her film had been accepted at Cannes but not understanding that she was actually expected to attend the festival in person:[62]

> "This is Pierre Rissient you don't know me, but I am this guy from Cannes and may I have permission to take your films?" And this is out of the blue. Cannes. I didn't even know about it really.

> I just said. "Yes, thank you very much. Thank you for your kind comments." And he said, "Well, it's in May" and I said, "Well, I won't be able to come because I'm on a holiday" and he said, "Ooh, but you have to come."[63]

As we know, in the end, Campion did go to Cannes where she met the festival's director Gilles Jacob, who later told the Australian Film Commission chair, Phillip Adams, "You must give her lots of money so she'll be in competition with a feature film in two years."[64] That first feature that she was invested in by the international film community would become *Sweetie*, a film that however was poorly received at Cannes. *A Girl's Own Story* is another short but one less successful than *Peel*. *A Girl's Own Story* can be called a comprehensively feminist and personal film, in which Campion even used a dress that belonged to her mother.[65] While lacking much mainstream appeal, it won the Rouben Mamoulian Award at the 1984 Sydney Film Festival with its portrayal of the fantasies of three young girls. In a famously hilarious scene, the protagonists Pam and Stella practice kissing but use cutouts of Ringo Starr and Paul McCartney to pretend they are not kissing each other. It is a feminist and personal film through and through, as Campion has said about it. This film will be analyzed in depth in my second chapter, as it constitutes, in my opinion, the core of Campion's directorial debut as auteur.

Campion's first feature, *2 Friends* from 1986, was also what we would call today a staunchly feminist film, as has been formulated by Gwendolyn Audrey Foster: "the film is resolutely and revolutionarily feminist, in the purest sense of the word; it's told entirely from a female perspective, and the men and boys who drift through the film are either weak, predatory, or as the girls describe them in one scene, 'hopeless.'"[66] Campion's next film—the 1989 feature *Sweetie*, co-written with Lee—"started with the idea of trying to talk about relationships that don't work, particularly relationships where people feel they're in love but it's not happening, or they feel they love but they don't want to have sex anymore."[67] While *2 Friends* and *Sweetie* will be a major focus of my second chapter, it is worth noting here that Campion was now a *filmmaker* and a starting auteur who could decide which story to tell, even if *Sweetie* did not get the desired response. In *Sweetie*, which Campion calls her most autobiographical film—in 1993, she remarked that the protagonist "Kay is the closest to how I was"—it is Dawn, a delusional young woman, who is in a dysfunctional family relationship.[68] Campion explains that the representation is supposed to be an imaginary world of family conflict. The character of *Sweetie* was inspired by a real man but, for family reasons and to protect his identity, she changed the character's gender: she departed from the real but still let the real be the "guide" to what is ultimately a fictional story. For the 1990 *An Angel at My Table*, adapted for television from Janet Frame's autobiography, Campion went back to her native New Zealand after living a while in Sydney where she had attended film school. Campion has always spoken very proudly of New Zealand, even at that time: "New Zealanders believe in modesty at all times and we all thought Australians were vulgar and coarse."[69] For this work, she was inspired by the operation of memory: "I wanted the first bits to be like little slides, visual impressions. [. . .] So I wanted Episode One to build up the storytelling with very short scenes that get longer and longer, as would a memory. By Episode Two, it's normal storytelling."[70]

In some of her other films, including *The Piano*, summarized above, Campion's women have different kinds of sexual drives and fantasies that also include an obsession with violence against women. Frannie Avery's character in *In the Cut*, a Brooklyn teacher played by Ryan, is sexually attracted to and obsessed with a police chief, played by Mark Ruffalo, who is trying to solve a series of brutal crimes against women by a serial killer, including the dismemberment of the victim's bodies. This obsession, where sexual lust and male violence meet, returns in the second season of *Top of the Lake*, where Detective Griffin, having returned to Sidney, is trying to stop a human-trafficking cartel. As mentioned above, *The Power of the Dog* holds a special and new position in Campion's oeuvre and I will be dedicating a full chapter to it, as well as to *Top of the Lake*, which will be discussed in the third chapter.

Overall, this survey has summarized some of Campion's most successful and well-known films while identifying certain feminist motives in them. I want to now give an account of the structure of the entire book. In Chapter 2, I will pay close attention to the construction of a transgressive gaze, the "feeling camera" in Campion's films. This is a gaze that highlights the marginalized, the excluded, both narratively and visually. The films analyzed in detail will be the early shorts *Peel*, *A Girl's Own Story*, and *After Hours*, and the mid-career features *Sweetie* and *Holy Smoke!* I won't be able to discuss *Bright Star* (2009) along with the short *The Water Diary* (2006) in any depth but will mention *Bright Star* briefly in the book's conclusion. The third chapter will start by returning to Campion's first feature film, *2 Friends*, to ask questions about female adolescent sexuality, and will then investigate the embodied feminist thought and female sexual desire in her Janet

Frame adaptation, *An Angel at My Table*, and her later films *The Piano* and *The Portrait of a Lady*. Chapter 4 will be centered on the question of how Campion rewrote some film genres from a traditionally masculine to a feminine voice: starting with the crime thriller *In the Cut*, which I will analyze in detail to a short description of the thriller TV series (*Top of the Lake*), and concluding with the Western genre (*Top of the Lake*). In this chapter, I will start asking why *In the Cut* was for some the most feminist and for others not a feminist film at all, similarly to the critiques she received for *The Piano*. The rest of the fourth chapter will be dedicated to Campion's methods of a feminist occupation and subversion of male-organized spaces with a series of feminist and activist interventions in contemporary art and politics. I will also briefly discuss a documentary, for which Campion was executive producer, *Abduction: The Megumi Yokota Story* from 2004, and point out its thematic ties to the origin story of *Top of the Lake*, which became the successful TV series for HBO. I will end with an in-depth discussion of *The Power of the Dog* and the question of rewriting the genre of the Western as female auteur. My fifth chapter will offer a positive conclusion to the main question of the book as a whole: Is Jane Campion a feminist auteur?

Before moving on to the individual chapters, I want to say some last general things about Campion as an auteur including some of her declared filmic influences that I find useful background. The Australian Film and Television School, where Campion studied, was also known to foster an auteurist climate that was influenced by French filmmaker François Truffaut, "in which the director often looked at his or her own life for inspiration."[71] In her speech honoring Lina Wertmüller at the Oscars, already discussed above, Campion cites the genius of Wertmüller's *Pasqualino Settebellezze*, calling the character of Pasqualino, played brilliantly by Giancarlo Giannini, beautifully controversial. Campion lists Pasqualino's flaws at length but also details his deeply troubling behaviors as a man: a rapist, a misogynist, and so on and so forth. From today's perspective, three years after this speech, her description of Pasqualino could almost fit Phil Burbank from *The Power of the Dog*, another unsympathetic character. While not a rapist, he is homophobic and misogynist, and cruel besides. As White points out: "In *The Power of the Dog*, Phil's brutality, misogyny, and his hidden homosexuality camouflaged by homophobia ultimately come from a place of secret, feminine vulnerability: he can care for the young man as Bronco Henry once cared for him."[72] This place is not unsimilar to that of Pasqualino from *Settebellezze*, who is shown as weak, vulnerable, and cruel at the same time. While I will be exploring Campion's revisionism of the Western format and its importance in my fourth chapter, worth remarking here is Campion's interest in cruel masculinity. As she says in an interview with Kisner in the New York Times, her interest is in the "hard marble" itself and how to create softness out of it.[73] She compares this operation to the sculptor Auguste Rodin whom she greatly admires.

Another influence Campion reveals throughout her career is the work of Peter Weir, representative of Australian New Wave cinema. Weir became a household name with his mystery drama *Picnic at Hanging Rock*, also from 1975, the same year as *Pasqualino Settebellezze*. The film, a milestone of 1970s cinema, was based on the 1967 novel by Joan Lindsay and tells the story of the unsolved mystery of the disappearance of several girls from a strict British-style boarding school in Victoria in 1900, when the girls head out on a picnic at a nearby mountain, called Hanging Rock, from which they never return. The historical reenactment of young women in a boarding school, their innocence, and their repressed sexuality—"life itself held back," as Weir calls it—and especially the way in which Weir produces a form of "poetic horror" all foreshadow Campion's *The Portrait of a Lady* as well as *The Power of the Dog*.[74] As I will discuss in Chapter 3, which is focused on women's sexual freedom in Campion's films, *The Piano* (1993), while influenced by such traditional costume films as *Picnic at Hanging Rock*, sets itself apart in terms of a traditional female gaze. Campion also mentions Spike Lee's films as an influence, as well as the "dirty secret" that she watches *The Godfather* at least once a year! Apart from these filmic influences, Campion's films have also been compared to Emily Brontë's 1847 novel, *Wuthering Heights,* published under the pseudonym Ellis Bell. Brontë's choice of pen name corresponded to other pseudonymous responses to the contemporaneous reception of women authors, as her sister Charlotte remembers in words that still resonate in the film industry today:

> We agreed to arrange a small selection of our poems, and, if possible, get them printed. Averse to personal publicity, we veiled our own names under those of Currer, Ellis, and Acton Bell; the ambiguous choice being dictated by a sort of conscientious scruple at assuming Christian names positively masculine, while we did not like to declare ourselves women, because—without at that time suspecting that our mode of writing and thinking was not what is

> called "feminine"—we had a vague impression that authoresses are liable to be looked on with prejudice; we had noticed how critics sometimes use for their chastisement the weapon of personality, and for their reward, a flattery, which is not true praise.[75]

Other literary influences are Jane Austen and Emily Dickinson, whom Michel Ciment suspected in 1989 was a reference for *The Piano*, ultimately confirmed by Campion herself.[76] One commonality among all her adapted films is the attention to detail that recalls these nineteenth-century authors, who, besides, were all women: "I like to start with details and get them right."[77]

A final postulate: for me, Jane Campion is a legacy woman auteur, whether my esteemed readers like the term or we don't, and her status as such was already confirmed before she won an Oscar for *The Power of the Dog*. In 2018, Campion compared the aftermath of #MeToo to the Berlin Wall falling: "It's like the Berlin Wall coming down, like the end of apartheid," she observes. "I think we have lived in one of the more ferocious patriarchal periods of our time, the '80s, '90s, and noughties. Capitalism is such a macho force. I felt run over."[78] This observation, prominent even at the time, foresaw Campion's own emergence as *the* woman filmmaker to in fact bring part of the wall down and not only follow the zeitgeist call to identify with the #MeToo movement. Campion has always been political and outspoken, but this book now furthers our understanding of her political and intellectual dimensions of her work by examining what each of her films have said in terms of a feminist philosophy of the characters and what film language has been used.

2

The Transgressive Gaze

Early Shorts and Mid-Career Features 1982–2009

Kaja Silverman, in her pivotal essay from 1988, "The Female Authorial Voice,"[1] states that all that can be known of an author would be expressed inside a text. The author inhabits the interior of the text. In alignment with post-structuralism, Silverman understands a text, or in the case of cinema, the film, as *the* expression of authorship. She reminds us of the pivotal discussion about authorship developed by Roland Barthes and other structuralists, for whom writing meant the death of the author by its iterability and "capacity to be reactivated in the absence of the writer."[2] According to the linguist and semiotician known for his important work in structuralist linguistics, Roman Jakobson (*Linguistics and Poetics*, 1960), the speech act is an "empty process," and happens in the absence of the writer. But what's important to Silverman and also to me in bringing back this reading of the "female authorial voice" is that the author's "new body" in the form of the text remains the support of a process that the structuralists coined *écriture*, writing. As already discussed in the previous chapter in relation to the review of the auteur theory, Silverman's idea is that a text or film expresses a writer's or director's literal *body* through their work and doesn't just produce a "text" through an "empty process" that is unrelated to a real person and a living body. The "author-as-scriptor," that is, the author written into the text itself, becomes the reborn author, who had been previously presumedly murdered by the text, in Barthes's *The Death of the Author* (1967). Silverman reminds us further that Barthes's very own later writing, *The Pleasure of the Text* (1973), redeems and brings back the body and flesh of the writer through their voice. Barthes replaces a "vocal writer" with the author he declared dead seven years earlier. This "vocal writing" is what Barthes links to the language of cinema.

But who was this dead author and who will be *his* reincarnation? This is where Silverman's chapter becomes interesting and her reading psychoanalytic, as she now interprets Barthes's *The Pleasure of the Text* as writing away a safe and firm gender identity that is, of course, placed in the normative male subject position that Barthes himself inhabits: "the author he seeks to annihilate occupies a definitely male position."[3] Silverman suggests, hence, that the former author, who is now dead, was male, and that the new writer who inhabits the text in lieu of this male author is androgynous, and that for this author inside the text "'woman' will be the preferred standard."[4] In other words, this newly obtained female authorship is built not only out of the textual reborn flesh and a constructed femininity itself, but it is built on the pillars of male castration. Connecting this point to the discussion about Sarris's auteurship from Chapter 1, Silverman reminds us of Andrew Sarris's lively account of this newborn author:

> Sarris envisions the auteur as both the origin and meaning of the cinematic text, insisting that there is a close relationship between the way an authored film "looks and moves," and the way its director "thinks and feels."[5]

Alistair Fox, in his opening lines to his well-known psychoanalytic reading of Jane Campion's entire oeuvre until *Bright Star* (2009), states that he wants to venture outside of the filmic text, and into the personal, since staying within the realm of the text:

> strikes me as unnecessarily limiting, not only because it detaches art from personal, social, and historical contexts, but also because, in so doing, it forecloses the possibility in identifying the formative roles of projection, identification, and evocation in cinematic creation—especially in instances, as in the case of Jane Campion, a great wealth of pertinent biographical information is available from "outside" the text.[6]

Just like Sarris, Fox believes that there is a "necessity of a personal element that connects to the director's own experience of life as the origins of genuine authorship."[7] Indeed, Fox looks outside of the filmic text to obtain information about the life experiences of the nuclear Campion family: Jane, her older sister Anna Campion, her parents Richard and Edith. I mentioned a few general things about Jane Campion's upbringing in Wellington, New Zealand. One additional relevant factor for the discussion of the below films dealing with marginalized characters and mental illness is Campion's experience with her own mother's depression. It wasn't until 1989 that Campion revealed publicly (in an interview with Sue Williams) that her mother suffered from depression and had to be hospitalized for this disease.[8]

Despite these problems, her relationship with both parents seems to have been positive and stayed active, and she involved each of them in her filmmaking in certain ways. In 1997, Edith Campion said proudly about her daughter: "If Jane hadn't done anything I think she may have become a great criminal. [. . .] She likes to set things in action and see what happens. But then, that's rather like being a movie director."[9]

While at times it feels intrusive, Fox's intentions toward his "patient Jane" are legitimate, as he is trying to make sense of her films and making them speak to one another, analyzing the creator behind them. While I will go back to Fox's specific readings of some of the films, particularly *Holy Smoke!* I want to already foreshadow his ultimate interpretation of the seat of Campion's authorship: from a childhood trauma of a "failed family romance," caused by the father's promiscuity and betrayal of the mother (including fathering an illegitimate child), an actress and writer, who became more and more depressed by her disappointment in her husband. Jane develops sexual fantasies of incest with the father to inhabit his subject position and control his actions, not as a daughter who is deprived of his fatherly love, but as a writer-director who can control and predict his actions. The dysfunctionality in the Campion family, says Fox, caused the parents to neglect their daughters, Anna (the older sister) and Jane. Instead of taking care of their daughters, the parents distracted themselves from their marital problems by making and producing theater together, and not dealing with the real-life issues. In a form of hyper-identification with the mother, according to "Dr. Fox," Jane took on the role of desiring the father, Richard, resulting, among other things, in a transgressive incestuous gaze expressed in her cinematic work. The dramatization of this unresolved family romance results in the works discussed in this chapter, particularly *Holy Smoke!* and later on *In the Cut*, which I discuss in Chapter 4.

Peel, 1982

As already summarized in Chapter 1, *Peel* is a family drama that tells the story of a family crisis taking place during a car ride, specifically the family of fashion designer Katie Pye. The actors playing father, mother, son all represent themselves in the film. As Dana Polan points out, referencing the subtitle of the film "An Exercise in Discipline," the film is about discipline in different ways:

> First, within the story of the film, characters strive for a self-discipline, a control of one's emotions in volatile situations: a brother and sister are trying not to explode; [. . .] the adults especially try to hold their anger in but instead of this self-discipline as being seen as a positive appeasement of familial tensions, it is shown (especially with the sister) as a form of repression and alienation: with their resentments welling inside but kept in check by passive exteriors, the characters become isolated, non-communicating figures fully given over to their separation from others.[10]

In this very first authorial work by Campion, on which she worked so hard that she had to be hospitalized,[11] but for which she was awarded the Palme d'Or for Best Short Film, and hereby in some ways launched her career, something relatively small and at first sight "irrelevant" is happening: an approximately ten-year-old looking boy with red hair and freckles is seated next to the father, who is driving the family car. Behind them sits the fashion designer and aunt, Katie Pye, playing the boy's sister, looking impatiently out the window, while dressed in a green jacket with embroidered white feathers. Underneath she is wearing a double-colored skirt in blue and pink, pink tights, and a yellowish multicolored flustered shirt. In one shot, when she has already taken off her green sweater and is standing in an angry posture beside the highway, her full figure appears a bit like a middle-aged Harlequin figure thanks to the double-colored skirt. The father's shirt design, which is brown and has red, orange, and white dots, equally gives a sense of irony and comedy, since his demeanor is all but "dotted." His pants are also patterned differently from his shirt entirely, in a light color scheme. The characters' discord and difference are clearly expressed by their dress code: everybody is wearing a different color and pattern, not only from each other but on their own bodies (Figure 4).

The family dissonance and resulting disagreement were first caused by the son, who peeled an orange in a provocative manner in the car,

FIGURE 4 Peel, *1982.*

throwing the peels out of the window, which then causes the father to stop the car and yell at the son outside of it, asking him to pick up the peels, which in turn causes the sister to run off frantically, and pee in the nearby woods, and complain that she will never make it back to town on time for an important meeting; in a climax of dissonance, the son runs into nearby bushes where he finds a condom and blows it up like a balloon; the domino effect is complete; visually, this family is, however, also represented in terms of their similarities and resemblances. In fact, it might be said that if there weren't so many visual communalities and repetitions on the screen, including the choice of the orange-colored orange that resembles all the characters' skin and hair tonalities, the drama would be less pronounced and also less satirical because it would not be perceived as a *family drama*. In *Peel*, every member is part and parcel of the same familial fabric. They are all intertwined and interdependent. In fact, toward the end of this 8:19 minute short, Campion lets us encounter the three protagonists' faces in extreme close-ups, which, taken out of the context of the story and the entirety of their faces, seem relaxed and indeed at peace with one another (Figures 5–8).

We are seeing these close-ups while inhabiting the point of view of the son (Figure 8), whose face, shifted to the side, shows us that it is he who is strolling his father's face with a gaze of inspection, and it is his questioning viewpoint that we are experiencing as viewers. It is precisely here that I would anchor Jane Campion's transgressive gaze, a gaze that comes from the youngest and most innocent of the three protagonists, the child. Through him, the film is asking: *Who are these people? Why is this my sister, why is this my father, and why do I owe them? Why am I with them*, and most importantly, *why do I need to*

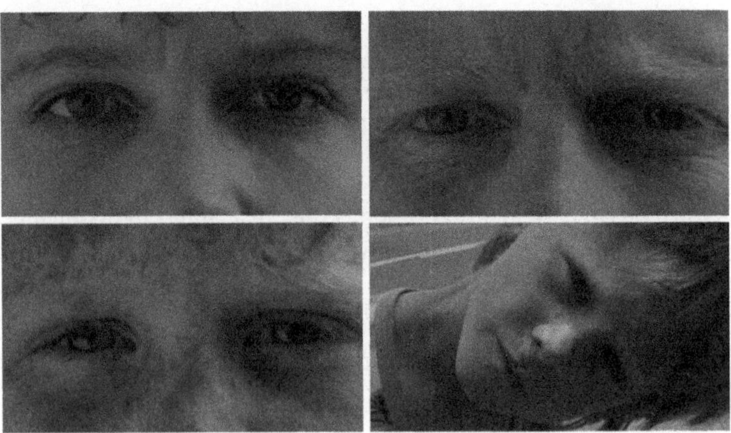

FIGURES 5, 6, 7, AND 8 Peel, *1982.*

obey and submit to them? Why am I not truly independent? The child's transgressive or forbidden action, peeling the orange and throwing its peels out the window, kicked off this family crisis, but it leads to the boy inspecting his own origin, his place in the world, trying to figure out what is wrong with his family and the world at large. To pack in such profound questions into a short film by a first-time filmmaker, it has to be said that this is a remarkable achievement.

Indeed, there is another "discipline" that Dana Polan talks about in his discussion of *Peel*, the one involved in being able to create a film language and *make* a film: "we can take the film itself to be a demonstration of the disciplined utilisation of established procedures of movie-making. [. . .] *Peel* is very much a work that wants emphatically to show off its discipline, its confident mastery of the rules of cinema production."[12]

Without venturing too far into a microscopic analysis of the film language employed by the young film student, Campion, in *Peel*, I do want to point out the use of two formal devices that will not leave her film language for the rest of her career: one is the art of composition, which for this film was the responsibility of the female cinematographer Sally Bongers, who was the first woman to shoot in 35mm in Australia, as already alluded to in Chapter 1. As Polan points out, the cinematography exhibits an intense play of foreground and background shots, whereby we see one person's position, for instance, the boy in the foreground and the father out of focus in the background, and then immediately followed by the reverse shot, with the father in the foreground and the boy out of field. These shots, which are created in great depth of field and edited in sequence, present a drastically changing world from each character's point of view, a change that is part of the human condition and remains unresolved. What is more, every character also only has a partial view of the world in his or her own way, a scale that is just theirs, which is expressed for instance in the opening montage of short shots following one another revealing a detail of a character's action via a constrained view: the boy playing with the orange with his feet up on the car's glove compartment giving us a partial view of his legs squeezed onto the left of the car, followed by a shot of the sister seated in the back, her head close against the right window, and behind her the green landscape passing by at a large scale, making her seem cramped.

To sum up, I want to reiterate that the transgressive gaze at work in *Peel* is playing harmoniously and in tune on all levels of the cinematic codes, just like Sarris would have imagined the "auteurial signature": the casting, the costumes, the actions, and the narration itself, and the visual rendering through the cinematographic composition of the world of a family crisis. Before continuing in my analysis of Campion's transgressive gaze developed in her other early film work, I want to briefly return to Fox's psychoanalytic reading of the "forbidden fruit" of the orange in *Peel.* Fox underscores the signification of the orange in the film as phallic image, evoking sexual intercourse:

> It seems to me that, at a deeply displaced and condensed symbolic remove, Peel is dealing with the same issue that is to be found in Campion's other short films: illicit sexuality, associated with the father, residing as a dark secret within the family, which cannot be acknowledged overtly and which produces simultaneously a fascination and aversion in the perspective offered by the filmmaker.[13]

Fox concludes in his usual patronizing style that it might be Jane Campion herself who is drawn toward the orange, this "fruit of knowledge," which she "fears ingesting."[14] While such a statement might be said for any coming-of-age film and the filmmaker behind it, the next three films, *A Girls' Own Story*, *After Hours*, and her first feature, *2 Friends*, will tell us much more about the status quo of female sexuality in Jane Campion's authorship through her own film language rather than through psychoanalytic speculation and interpretation.

A Girl's Own Story, 1984

Passionless Moments (1983) is technically the next short that Campion produced, a satire of everyday episodes, it was co-directed and written by her partner of the time, Gerard Lee, and based on Lee's more than Campion's life experience. I don't think this film aligns itself well with the transgressive gaze currently highlighted in this chapter because, as many have noted, its base is silliness and surrealism. While this overall tone can, of course, be counted as transgressive, the filmic approach is too experimental to compare well with other narrative films under analysis. As Polan notes, it does have a very interesting opening that I will reference in the below discussion of *An Angel at My Table.*[15]

A Girl's Own Story positions itself into the lineage of what Mark Stiles has called "representations of problems in the construction of girls' identities."[16] As Dana Polan has it, these problems are laid out on the table very concretely and dramatically, without any holding back: "This is a film whose story deals with real-life crises that young adolescent girls can confront—sexual confusion family strife, incest (a girl made pregnant by her brother), molestation (the young heroine dragged into a car by a mysterious man)."[17]

The film is, in a certain way, the director's own story, as it bears strong autobiographical references from Campion's upbringing and life at home, including the storyline of the mother, played by Australian model and actress Colleen Fitzpatrick, who suffers from depression due to her husband's overt marital infidelity; a fact that is a direct quotation from Jane Campion's personal childhood memories of her father Richard cheating on her mother Erica. The mother character in the film is even wearing Jane Campion's mother's own dress, as shown in the below stills. This fact created a lot of talk at the time of the film's release when Anna, Jane Campion's sister, discovered the family connections in it. In an interview published in the Sydney Daily Telegraph, Jane Campion revealed: "'Mum never noticed,' until my sister said, 'Don't you see. We're all in that film'"[18](Figures 9 and 10).

FIGURES 9AND 10 A Girl's Own Story, *1984.*

As Alistair Fox summarizes, in his usual manner of psychoanalyzing Campion through her filmmaking, "*A Girl's Own Story* has the story of Edith Campion and her troubled marriage at its center."[19] However, it might be added that the marriage crisis resolves in an unrealistic transgressive scene at the end of the film, where the parents start having sex in front of their daughters' eyes, breaking the ultimate family taboo. As Fox points out in his reading of *The Piano* (see Chapter 3), the muteness of the mother bears a resemblance with Ada's muteness and her state of repression coming from a Scottish puritanical society and being under cultural shock when she first arrives in colonized Maori's New Zealand (Figure 11).

In my short analysis, I want to focus not on the parents but on the main protagonist, the young girl Pam, and her friends, including sister Prue, who are all transitioning from childhood to girlhood and adolescence inside a dysfunctional family setting. The film starts in a Catholic school setting: in the school courtyard, we see close-ups of girls yelling out of the depth of their lungs and singing hysterically to a Beatles song, while dressed and dancing in classic school uniforms. It is said that these uniforms were also the ones Jane and her sister Anna wore when they were children. The film tells a

FIGURE 11 A Girl's Own Story, *1984.*

sequence of episodes in "a girl's life," all transgressive in nature, and presented in sequence accompanied by the recurring music box version of Doctor Zhivago's "Somewhere, My Love," underscoring a feeling of irony. One is the famous episode of Pam with her friend Stella in Pam's bedroom. The girls are testing out how it might feel to be kissed by a Beatle (from the band *The Beatles*), using cutouts of Ringo Starr and Paul McCartney, a scene for which Nicole Kidman was cast but refused the role because of having to kiss a girl. Another one is brother Graeme and sister Gloria, who are seen playing kittens, taking off their clothes, which leads them to realize Graeme's idea of having incestuous sex (off-screen). That story arc ends with Gloria at a home for unmarried women run by nuns, having to give up the baby for adoption. Brother Graeme is present, and when asked to kiss his sister, he answers cynically, "it's not proper." A third one is Pam's birthday, when her father's girlfriend Deidre suddenly takes part in a dinner celebration that was supposed to happen just between the father and daughter. Pam, whose identity is based on Jane's, and Prue's on Anna's, shows a "complexity of attitude" that might be linked to the "possibility that, as a young child, she suffered sexual abuse."[20] Fox's comprehensible deduction stems from another scene, where little Pam is lured into a car by a male driver, whose shoes and hands are the only things we ever see, offering her to pet a kitten, and luring her into his car. Whether this scene was based on a real event or not, the film as such results in what Fox calls a blend of "excitement and fear regarding sexuality." Another reading of the last scene might be a city myth and the sentence said by many mothers to their daughters, "don't ever step into anybody's car even if there is a little kitten; or, don't take candy from strangers." Whether or not such a scene was lived by the individual, it exists as a narrative in a "girl's upbringing."

While these storylines are shocking per se, they aren't alone in constructing the transgressive gaze in this film. So how is the transgressive gaze constructed in *A Girl's Own Story*? Already the emblematic, if not iconic opening scene, before the opening credits, of a group of girls looking at a biology book of drawings of male genitalia is constructed through a "feeling camera" that presents only first person views including a haptic shot of the girls touching the genitalia in question. Under the drawing, the caption reads: "This sight may shock young girls" (Figure 12).

This "feeling camera" operated, once again, by Sally Bongers, testifies to a situation through the characters' varied point-of-view shots, a gaze that becomes capable of positioning itself from within the family members and girlfriends, picking up their intimate moods and feelings. But the "feeling camera" isn't the only way to get the

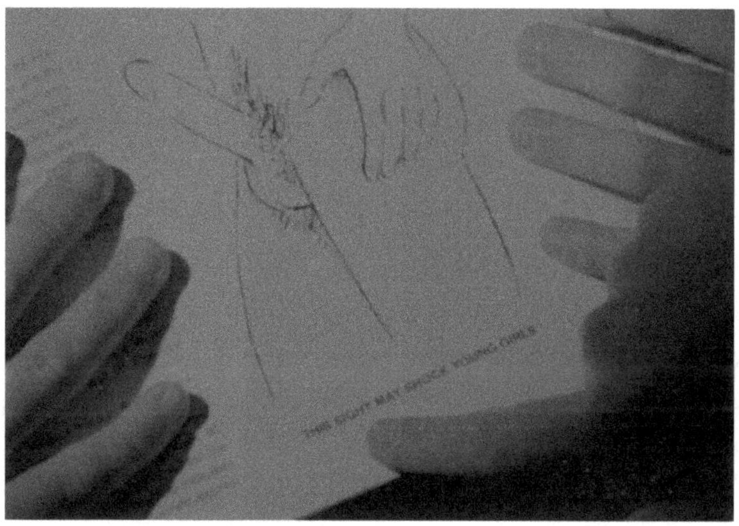

FIGURE 12 A Girl's Own Story, *1984.*

viewer attached to the film. As opposed to *Peel*, the protagonists let us look inside of them and experience their inner lives. The dialogue is often funny but also revealing. For instance, the parents don't speak to each other directly, but through their daughters. During an oppressive feeling family dinner, the mother asks one of her daughters to ask, "who he was out with so late last night." When the mother suddenly leaves the dinner table and the girls start blaming their father, he says: "You watch yourself. She is my wife and I love her." We obtain a psychological knowledge of the characters through Campion's script and her direction. As a result, we feel a family's dysfunctionality under our own skin, and, more importantly, we start to care about it. The film feels *lived*, whether this is "real life" or memories, but one has the impression the filmmaker, and through her the film, is testifying something and that the stories told aren't simply exercises in filmmaking any longer but have meaning beyond the screen.

Another thing pointed out by other film critics, such as Dana Polan, is the fact that while the tackiness of the characters in *Peel* made us feel a bit distant from them and experience their dysfunctional family as a case study or an "exercise" as stated above, *A Girl's Own Story* is a story we can relate to and live *with* the characters. With the personalized title, Campion also introduces a narrative that can be compared to a form of what film scholar Michael Renov has called a "domestic ethnography," to describe a truthful and authentic cinematically created relationship of the filmmaker with their family members who they put in display.[21] While Renov analyzes documentaries, the cinematic techniques employed to create the lived experience are, of course, not limited to the documentary genre. Through the creation of domestic intimacy in *A Girl's Own Story*, the viewer gets the feeling of: "Someone gave us permission to be there." Or "This someone must have the authority to do so as they have lived what we see on screen." With this feeling, we not only have permission to engage in the drama but can deeply relate and believe its cinematic truth. The difficult and personal content, that is, the themes of transgression, incest, adultery, and adolescent sexual awakening, are thereby placed behind the main judgment-free experience of a truthful encounter with a world created by the filmmaker. While Campion wanted to feature Nicole Kidman in the role of Pam, as mentioned above, she had to wait until *The Portrait of a Lady* until she would be able to work with her, as these difficult themes were too controversial for the young Australian star of the time. Interestingly, the opening montage sequence of *The Portrait of a Lady* will bear a strong resemblance with the end sequence of *A Girl's Own Story*, as I will discuss in Chapter 3.

After Hours, 1984

A young woman, Lorraine, reports the sexual abuse by her superior, John Phillips, in an undescribed office job. Lorraine says it happened during "after hours" work sessions that Mr. Phillips, "a weird guy," forced her into. The opening shows us Lorraine in psychologist Sandra Adams's office. The attractive woman is conducting this investigation of the sexual harassment complaint in a serious and, at times, dispassionate fashion, seeming in disbelief of Lorraine, and challenging her with uncomfortable allegations, "why she did not refuse the offer more drastically, and how come she did not see it coming." Under this pressure, Lorraine admits that she was confused and was unable to act appropriately at the time. Throughout the film, we see flashbacks of what truly happened between Lorraine and Mr. Phillips and learn that everything she said to the investigator is correct. We also see how all the people involved in her life, including her mother, but also the people in the offender's world, such as his wife, Mrs. Phillips, or his secretary, or Lorraine's co-workers, are supporting the negation of the sexual offense, but do so in a disturbingly innocent, almost frivolous manner. What is more, Lorraine's memories are at times contradicting each other, and she herself falls into a form of resignation, stating to her mother, "I'd rather forget the whole thing." As a result of this unstable narrative, unstable only to the character Lorraine, as the viewer did see the truth with their own eyes, the investigator suggests to Lorraine, who has meanwhile lost her job, to drop the case. A depressing ending for a film about sexual harassment in the workplace.

There is truth about *After Hours*, that the film is to a certain extent "anti-feminist," as Dana Polan has pointed out: "Women in *After Hours* do not stand up for other women."[22] Besides, a lot of the film's twenty-five minutes not only gives too much airtime to the offender, whose abusive actions and sexual harassment we see deliberately on-screen, but it also creates a world of "anti-heroines," who are not only lacking solidarity but are either silent and passive bystanders (such as her own mother, who even accuses her of wearing a mini-skirt and by that potentially self-inflicting the sexual trespassing), or, just like the investigator, are disbelievers in Lorraine's narrative (such as the swimming trainer or Mr. Phillips's secretary). Nobody is doing anything about the abuse, and even Lorraine herself becomes an "anti-heroine" when she herself wants to drop the ball.

It does feel frustrating as if Campion made a consciously anti-empowering film with a negative anti-ending that even carries a sarcastic undertone with it, when the anti-heroine figure of the uncompassionate secretary wanders around the empty office, wondering what to do with Lorraine's remaining chicken in the fridge that has now gone bad after her dismissal. On the other hand, one could say that by showing the reality of most narratives of public allegations of sexual harassment, Campion pointed her finger at the true problem of sexual harassment and its mediatization, by highlighting the question of "proof" and the question of a "reliable memory," which is often obfuscated to the victim due to dissociation.[23] In other words, something we only learned after 2017 with the sexual harassment awareness campaign #MeToo, we now know that in most cases, victims are not believed and therefore drop the case, which attributes to a high sense of realism in *After Hours*. Bystanding, bad-mouthing behind Lorraine's back in the workplace, the lack of community at home, these are the themes that account for a sense of transgression in *After Hours*. Instead of making an empowerment film about sexual harassment, and indeed refusing to make such a film "that says how one should or should not behave,"[24] as Campion puts it herself, she made a film about the transgressions of the society around someone who has been abused and transgressed against. I would say that such a film is indeed more interesting and complex than the "empowerment film" that explains what the right behavior might be in the face of sexual harassment and speaks the language of a classic "activist" film.[25]

While it is true that the film incorporates some contrived dialogue, as already mentioned in Chapter 1, which was the result of its commission by the Women's Film Unit of Film Australia and that consequently Campion did not have full control over the film, calling it a "film with a purpose"[26] with some resentment. Nevertheless, *After Hours* contains the handwriting of Campion and some of the very stylized Campion shots of a girl's world and girls' group activities, wearing school uniforms or swimsuits in this case, that we have already seen in her earlier shorts such as *Tissues* and *A Girl's Own Story*. The underwater swimming shots (Figure 13), to which we arrive by shock cut after the uncomfortable opening sequence in the investigator's office, for instance, literally immerse us into the innocent community of girls and into the life of a happy Lorraine, who by contrast to the earlier scene in the investigator's office, is shown as a young athlete in control of her body. We might say that Campion's critique of sexual harassment lies in her choice of imagery, the film language itself, and less in what is said on-screen.

FIGURE 13 After Hours, *1984.*

In this scene, where we see the girls' legs swimming underwater, there is a poetic innocence that arises by watching these paddling legs, foreshadowing the importance of the poetic role of the water in *The Piano*. We "witness" a sense of unspoken community, which can only be intact underwater, where other people including adults and particularly men aren't admitted, nor have the right to touch it or aestheticize it. With this sequence of underwater shots that immerse us poetically in the world of the protagonist, Campion says it all and doesn't need a lengthy narrative explanation. I would say that the entire film's richness and originality is rooted in this language of "complicated patterns and bold editing,"[27] which includes the use of pop or shock colors used for Lorraine's and other girls' accessories (lipstick, goggles, skirt, bright green walls, etc.), a strongly contrasting composition style with stark variations of field of depth that have already appeared in *Peel*, as well as a disjunctive storytelling technique (which in *2 Friends* will indeed become a reverse timeline)—rather than a linearly scripted dialogue, or even a linear overall plot itself.

Lorraine's discomfort over her unresolved harassment case and the fact that she can't communicate her inner turmoil to others are reflected in the film language of striking composition, stark contrasting color scheme, contrasting fore and backgrounds and less in the acting and dialogue. What we come out of is the story of a woman who has been objectified twice over: by her superior who takes advantage of his power position, and by the world around her who ignores or simply doesn't see and acknowledge her real inner life. The exposed individual as an object of public discussion who encounters no solidarity and cannot find help will thread itself throughout many, if not all of Campion's films, as Dana Polan so aptly points out. In this helpless exposure and the resulting solitude, I agree with Alistair Fox, who detects a "suicidal ideation" in Lorraine, as in one of the final scenes she touches the surface of the water in a swimming pool, "making concentric circles on it, and then allows herself to fall into the pool's depths, causing the viewer to wonder whether she intends to drown herself."[28] Lorraine's suicidal drive in *After Hours* and some of the underwater imagery are a hint at Ada's character in *The Piano*, and her attempt at letting herself drown together with her piano at the very end of the film. I will return to this topos in the next chapter's detailed discussion of *The Piano*.

Dana Polan made another important connection between *After Hours* and such later films as the indie classic *Sweetie*, discussed below, or the world successes of *An Angel at My Table* and *The Piano*. All of these films demanded a "designed film language."[29]

Sweetie, 1989

Sweetie isn't the main character of *Sweetie*, but as Campion says, "it was a pretty title, not because she is the heroine of the story."[30] It is the story of two sisters, Kay (Karen Colston) and "Sweetie," who is actually called Dawn (played by the legendary Geneviève Lemon, who will be working with Campion up until *The Power of the Dog*), who couldn't be more different, yet they share the same family and the problems within it. Sweetie believes she is a hot actress when in real life she is delusional, aggressive, and completely dysfunctional. Kay is a pretty factory worker who falls in love with Louis (Tom Lycos, who was chosen for his resemblance to co-writer Gerard Lee, from whom Campion was separated but continued working with), but soon will fall out of love with him. He will eventually leave her. Kay's factory work world resembles Lorraine's office world from *After Hours*, where she was talked about behind her back and where nobody stood up for her. But Kay's world is quirky and her co-workers are depicted as spoofs and not just as mean people, and there is no moral judgment about them (Figure 14).

When Gordon and Flo, the parents, who are usually fighting and estranged from one another, decide to go on a trip together, leaving the difficult one, Sweetie, back, things turn to the dark side. What is more, they can no longer ignore, as they have until now, their daughter's mental illness. *Sweetie* is the first film that Campion finishes after her acclaimed and prize-winning shorts at the Cannes Film Festival. When she is asked if there is a difference between her shorts and *Sweetie*, she answers Michael Ciment:

FIGURE 14 Sweetie, *1989.*

> Not really. Except Sweetie is the best and the strongest film I've done. It's a film that I controlled the least, which brought me where I didn't really know I was going, and in this sense it was a great adventure. In this sense I was very satisfied.[31]

Cannes' programmer, Pierre Rissient, who had first invited Jane Campion's short films and gave her the first platform for international recognition, was also responsible for selecting *Sweetie* at Cannes. The film's premiere at Cannes, however, was a setback, and some journalists called it even a disastrous screening. For sure it polarized the audience. Campion fans started comparing her to David Lynch and Jim Jarmusch,[32] hence, attributing a unique voice and auteurship to her. In this sense, the film was a success and, of course today it's one of several classic Campion films, not to mention that it won many awards among which an American Film Institute for best screenplay. Campion wrote and developed *Sweetie* during a time when she was also preparing and writing her two later films, *The Piano* and *An*

Angel at My Table. The reason for *Sweetie* to come into the world before them, as Campion stated, was that the financing of *Sweetie* came together very fast and sort of accidentally.[33]

The film was co-written with her former boyfriend Gerard Lee, with whom she continued a professional relationship (and seventeen years later would also co-write the *Top of the Lake* TV series discussed in Chapter 4). The character of Sweetie was in fact based on one of Lee's family members' experiences, who was a man, but Campion and Lee changed the gender to make the family member unrecognizable. The story, while fictional, is inspired by real family conflict in both writers' families (Gerard Lee's mother had recently separated from the father, and Campion's parents had already divorced in 1984) and by Campion's interest in dysfunctional family dynamics in general, to say it with her own ironic words: "families can be incredibly funny at times and yet there is a tragic underbelly."[34] As Fox points out, Campion was particularly preoccupied with relationships that didn't work, or even failed. As with *A Girl's Own Story*, many of the narrative threads were drawn directly from her own life.

> It started off being about a couple—myself and the co-writer on "Sweetie," Gerard Lee—and the problems of feeling like we were in love but not having the relationship work.[35]

As we know from many more interviews and public statements by Campion, she likes reality to guide her, and of course, many directors and writers do so. But with *Sweetie*, Campion wanted to make a film "that had more interior to it, because I think we all have an interior life [. . .] What's happening inside is so big for you, yet on the surface you are making cups of tea."[36] This is also what made her open the film with a voice-over:

> With Kay's voice-over, we wanted to indicate from the start that we weren't only interested in what the characters do but also in what they think and feel.[37]

Kay is indeed the main character of *Sweetie* and not Sweetie, and as Campion states below, she feels the most connection with her character Kay, and in that sense, *Sweetie* is the most autobiographical of Campion's films thus far. For instance, Campion based Sweetie's horse collection on her own sister Anna's. In fact, she also dedicated the film to her sister, which Anna allegedly felt uncomfortable about: "I don't really appreciate you stealing hunks of my personality and mixing it up with this nutcase. And not exactly expressing to the press that it's nothing to do with me."[38] When asked about how much Campion projects herself into her characters (including Ada and Janet Frame from her later films), she gives this interesting response to Michael Ciment and Thomas Bourguignon:

> I don't think I project my fantasies in these characters, and in any case I don't know who I am. We are what we do. On the other hand, I have a lot of tenderness for them, even if none of them represent me, though Kay is the closest to what I was.[39]

The first part of the film is focused on Kay's inner life, a depressed and quirky factory worker falling in love with Louis, even though he is dating one of her best friends, and she has to convince him to go with her. Soon thereafter, Kay becomes undecided about her feelings for Louis and turns the relationship into a brother-sister kind of situation with separate rooms in the same house. As Fox points out in his psychoanalytic reading of Kay's behavior, she turns the situation into a fake incest taboo, whereby it feels "wrong" to her to have sex. When the couple is shown together, they are having sleepovers like best friends rather than sex. Fox also points out that Kay's frigidity and later on Ada's sexual repression in *The Piano* are already prefigured by Pam and Prue's sexual preoccupations and activities in *A Girl's Own Story*.[40] But below I will go into a closer reading of this "frigidity" and separate it from a psychoanalytic assumption that women *must* desire (men) (Figure 15).

Sweetie, for her part, perceives herself as a sex bomb breakthrough actress and constantly makes love to her boyfriend Bob, an imaginary "manager," who is in truth a *dolce far niente* drug addict, right next to her sister's room. Kay, who is driven insane by the vulgar sex noises next door, desperately knocks at Sweetie's door to make her stop. In addition to being a sex fanatic and delusional, she is also abusive: she destroys her sister's clothes, she breaks furniture, and she pees out in

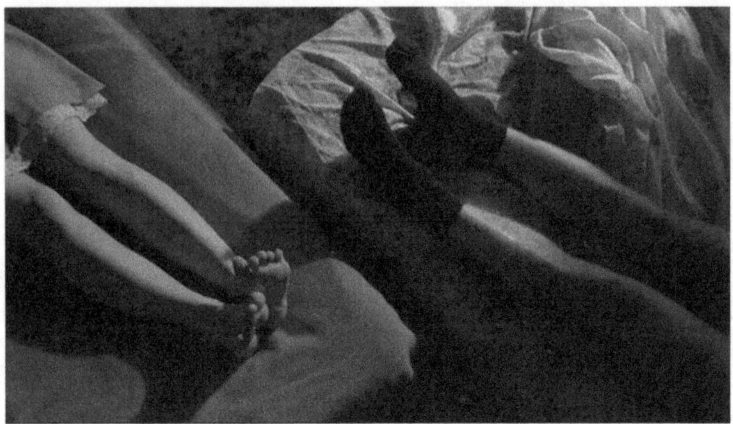

FIGURE 15 Sweetie, ***1989.***

the open. The fighting between the sister characters Dawn (Sweetie) and Kay was apparently based on a smaller scale on some of Jane Campion's own fights with her sister Anna.[41] At any rate, it is clear that Campion wanted to make a film with a *provocative* point of view, as she says it, showing dysfunctionality in its fullest display (unlike *Peel* that only hinted at it in comparison), and she knew that this film had to be made before some of the other ones with a more dramatic and even tragic tonality, such as *An Angel at My Table* and *The Piano*. *Sweetie* and *Holy Smoke!*, discussed next in this chapter, on the other hand, are not made with a fully compassionate tonality or serosity,[42] and maybe the lack thereof is what makes these films all the more profound.

I want to direct my focus on the film's transgressive nature that often departs from a sexual narrative per se, such as Kay not wanting it or Sweetie being a sex maniac. The transgressions in *Sweetie*, in my opinion, are all about transgressions within one family, where literally every family member transgresses their ethical boundaries. Sweetie's transgressions don't serve the female characters' inner worlds to find a liberated sexual fantasy or even an active sex life, as many of Campion's later female lead characters (Ruth, Ada, Jane), but I believe that they serve to display the problem of the family as such, and the fact that it is a system of codependency and coproduction. Everybody in this system is also responsible for the other, and if one person is dysfunctional, it will affect all other ones, as well. In fact, the film's culmination occurs when the three family members return to Sweetie, whom they had left behind. Sweetie, in a lunatic act of revolt, gets completely naked, curses her family with the worst names, colors her body black, and climbs up her old tree house in the backyard. She falls from the tree, injuring her mom Flo. Not to mention that she also kills herself. In her final voice-over narration, Kay says, "Trees never seem to leave us alone." I agree with Fox, who seems to imply that the "legacy of the dysfunctional family might continue to disturn the mental well-being of its members."[43] Considering that, as Fox is informed, Edith Campion attempted suicide during the final weeks of Sweetie's production, we can assume that the family system that Campion was informed by was her own, as well, and not just Gerald Lee's family members. Mental illness, the main theme of Sweetie, is therefore seen as something produced by family members and their actions. It is the result of a collective and not an individual problem.

In conclusion, I want to say a few words about the visual environment and this world in which mental illness is at home: shot again by Sally Bongers with a garish palette while at the same time affecting a drab realism, Sweetie intended to make one uncomfortable in its bittersweet depiction, particularly its sly intimation of father-daughter incest. Bongers' camerawork is characterized by an unconventional visual approach, often changing camera-angles, which can be seen as reflecting Campion's own rebellious personality.[44] Certainly, the smart set at Cannes, where it debuted, slammed their seats in disgust, though the more discerning put the film on the map.[45] The film stands out also through the use of a cappella music, for which Campion had the idea early on. She knew she wanted to hear human beings singing, which ended up being the voices of an Australian white gospel group of thirty singers called Café at the Gate of Salvation. All but the last song, which Campion took from a book of Jewish prayers, was theirs. The last song, the iconic love song, "Love Me with All Your heart": "Love you with all my heart as I love. Don't give me your heart for a moment or an hour. . . . Love me always as you've loved me. . . . With every beat of your heart." We hear the song performed by the young Sweetie dressed up in pink as a little girl, through the point of view of the father, who starts hearing the song from behind the tree, and as he moves closer into camera and we see him frontally, we get closer to the little girl, who performs in a concentrated manner as the tree's branches are moving in and out. Through the ambivalence of this end scene, and the father's viewpoint, Campion seems to say that this family is broken, and Sweetie's death is the death of their family romance. Just like in *After Hours*, Sweetie's family did not stand by their daughter but left her behind.

When *Sweetie* was playing in competition at Cannes, Campion admits to feeling dwarfed by "the big boys" like Fred Schepisi (*Evil Angels*). *Sweetie* was completely ignored in the list of award winners, and *Sex, Lies, and Videotape* took all the attention. The jury was headed by Wim Wenders with the task of spotlighting a very personal first feature of modest budget. Certainly, *Sweetie* was exactly that, but at the time, the director's club of all (white) men did not recognize Campion as one of theirs. She would have to wait more than thirty years for that to happen. Today, *Sweetie* is a classic, and Pierre Rissient, the programmer at Cannes, a hero. After inviting her to screen her short films and *Sweetie*, he was also instrumental in finding Campion the money to produce *The Piano*.

Holy Smoke! 1999

Jane Campion had the idea for the film reportedly on a trip back from India, where she had vacationed, and was wondering about the status quo of spirituality and how one "falls" for it: "I wanted to make a contemporary film and just explore the subject of spirituality and the confusion about it."[46] Its birth lies between an earlier story that Campion had written called *Big Shell* (and was never made into a film),[47] and the homonymous novel that Jane Campion wrote with her sister Anna Campion.[48] The story itself was supposed to be based on Christopher Isherwood's autobiography, *My Guru and His Disciple* (1980), but in an interview with Michel Ciment, Campion revealed that she wasn't able to produce a script that satisfied her.[49] Instead, she wrote the film together with her sister Anna Campion, an actress, writer, and filmmaker in her own right. In an interview with the Australian TV news program ABC 7:30, Jane Campion says that the ambiguity of the status quo of spirituality in *Holy Smoke!* came from the fact that the two sisters had a completely different approach to belief and spirituality. While Jane wanted to find reasons to believe, Anna was completely agnostic.[50] The film was produced by Miramax and had a prominent cast of top-rated actors with Kate Winslet and Harvey Keitel in the lead, two actors whose appearances in the successful films *Titanic* (1997) for Winslet and *The Piano* (1993), *Pulp Fiction* (1994), and *From Dusk Till Dawn* (1996) for Keitel were still fresh on people's minds. I want to mention, too, that the members from the US religious cult Heaven's Gate, had committed mass suicide in 1997, only two years before the release of *Holy Smoke!*, which made the film very topical at the time of its release.

As film critics and scholars have pointed out before me, *Holy Smoke!* creates a whimsical, quirky universe, and an ambiguous lightness of tone that Campion's two previous films, *The Piano* (1993) and *The Portrait of a Lady* (1996), had departed from as they engaged with a deeper emotionality and perhaps intellectuality. For reasons I have explained earlier, I have situated these two previous films, which Campion made between *An Angel at My Table* and *Holy Smoke!* in the next chapter, which thematizes the female body, its autonomy, and especially female sexuality. I believe that *Holy Smoke!* is one Campion film that would technically fit into both categories that Chapters 2 and 3 examine at large: transgression and female sexuality. But I have kept it here in Chapter 2 with the focus on transgression, which is expressed in the film's satirical tone because I believe that that's its key theme that keeps all other themes, and even the main one about cults and religious leaders, interconnected. For me, *Holy Smoke!* is a film about transgression and taboos, in particular the incestuous fantasy of the sexual act between a daughter and a father, explored through the external story of an Indian cult leader and his follower. I say "external" because the story of the cult leader actually doesn't have much to do with what is really at play here: confronting the father figure. In other words, this film is about overcoming and transgressing father figures starting with the Indian cult leader Baba (meaning father) Chidaatma, followed by the cult exit counselor PJ (played by Harvey Keitel), followed by the figure of Gilbert Barron, Ruth's, that is, the heroine's own father and her macho brothers. All of these father figures are representatives of what Campion and Campion, in their novel, call "cunt men," men who read porno magazines, are drenched in vanity and self-obsession, are not able to love women for who they are, and are only interested in women as sexually consumable objects. Not least "cunt men" are also liars to their wives and children, have secret extramarital affairs, and father illegitimate children, as in the case of Ruth's father Gilbert Barron in *Holy Smoke!* as well as Richard Campion, Jane and Anna Campion's real father, as "Dr. Fox" points out. The film's resulting overall point that I am left with is that a young, emotional woman like Ruth manages to escape and overcome patriarchy, represented through these powerful and evil male figures, only by *transgression*, and I will return to this point in detail below.

As Alistair Fox points out, *Holy Smoke!* was influenced visually and in style by Bernardo Bertolucci's *Last Tango in Paris* from 1972. In my opinion, it is also the film that visually foreshadows *The Power of the Dog*, a revisionist Western, and I believe that both of these films are also responses, both critical and satirical, to patriarchy's "natural order," which gets distorted through wide lenses framing these specific landscapes as way bigger than our eyes could ever see, like in a tourist postcard. The landscape of the Flinders Ranges in South Australia, where *Holy Smoke!* takes place at *Mount Emu Farm*, and at *Half Way Hut*, where Ruth has been taken against her will to be "de-programmed" from the cult, has a strong visual resemblance with the dramatic location of Central Otago in New Zealand's South Island, where *The Power of the Dog* (2021) was filmed to represent 1925 Montana, USA. I will come back to this point later in Chapter 4 (Figure 16).

Holy Smoke! tells the story of a strong-willed young woman from Mt. Emu Farm, Australia, Ruth Barron (played by Kate Winslet), who falls under the spell of a charismatic religious guru Baba Chidaatma during her travels in India. Her family back in Australia, who is depicted as a stereotypically uneducated but very loving Australian family living in the Outer Banks, often depicted to produce comic relief, is desperately trying to get Ruth back

FIGURE 16 Holy Smoke! *1999.*

home, to save her. Because Ruth is brainwashed, it takes the faking of a medical emergency by her father to actually make her fly back home. Once Ruth returns to Mt. Emu Farm in Wee Waa, Australia, her parents hire a cult de-programmer called PJ Waters (played by Harvey Keitel), who looks and behaves like a charismatic macho. Not surprisingly, instead of getting Ruth out of the cult, PJ, who is twice Ruth's age, falls in love with her. This is not his only sexual relationship on-screen, as PJ also entertains a relationship with her sister-in-law, Yvonne, a hypersexualized young woman who seduces him during a car ride before he starts his "work" with Ruth in the *Half Way Hut*. In a post #MeToo era, we can comfortably label PJ as a man who consciously takes advantage of his power and enters into an abusive sexual relationship with the young Ruth, his presumed "patient," who is not only half his age but also mentally unstable and immature. Even though it was Ruth who took the first step and seduced PJ, it is clear from the storyline that her mental state wasn't such to make an informed decision, and therefore the "consensuality" of this relationship remains problematic in terms of the unequal distribution of age and power. But Ruth abuses the cult exit counselor PJ in her own right, not only by submitting him to emotional games of falling-in-love-rituals ("I love you, no I don't love you anymore") but also by giving him meticulous directions for performing for her, for instance, kissing her properly ("don't open your mouth too wide") and ultimately objectifying him into her own personal sex tool. In one of the final scenes before the relationship collapses, PJ's assistant Carol (played by Pam Grier) arrives unannounced *at Half Way Hut* tries to save her boss from his own trespassing and Ruth's sex fantasies. PJ sends her away, only to be cross-dressed by Ruth, who is busy putting makeup on him, combing him, and putting his hair into a hairband—as if he was her doll—playing out a sort of role-reversal fantasy. As I will discuss further in Chapter 3, particularly in my reading of *The Piano* and *The Portrait of a Lady*, Campion's male hero characters are often shown as feminized, which plays out here in PJ's cross-dressing, having turned this man into a feminized object of desire for the female heroine and her sexual pleasure. At this point in the film, what feels like that a comedy about the sexual power dynamics and codependencies between a cultish male guru or cult exit counselor and a female follower/victim has turned into a serious drama about a young woman's own confusion about her (sexual) desires. Accordingly, on IMDB, the film is in fact labeled as both comedy and drama. In this scene, Ruth takes the transgression one step further and performs like a dominatrix and forces to look at himself in the mirror "in order to present him with a mirror image of his undesirability. PJ's humiliation is complete when she forces

FIGURE 17 Holy Smoke!, *1999.*

him to recognize that he is a 'dirty old man.'"[51] As Alistair Fox points out, there is an element of sadism in this scene, through which we get a sense not only of reversal of roles but of revenge, which is reminiscent of a certain role-play performed in sexual fantasies. Jane Campion comments on this scene in her own words that make the reversal of roles crystal clear (Figure 17):

> She acts toward PJ out of full force of knowing what it is to be sexually objectified: to only be seen in terms of one's own beauty—which in some way, is not to be seen at all. This is why she dresses him up in the red dress, so that when he looks at himself he is seeing a woman his own age, someone sexually undesirable. She wants to appal him with his own double standard.[52]

It is no surprise that Alistair Fox, in his psychoanalytic account of Campion's film work, is particularly interested in the status quo of the sexual fantasies played out in *Holy Smoke!*

> *Holy Smoke* bears all the hallmarks of a sexual fantasy that has been concretized and made explicit, both in its structure and in the nature of the psychological mechanisms that are depicted as being at work in its action.[53]

Anna Campion revealed that writing the script for *Holy Smoke!* with her sister felt at times "verging on family therapy."[54] Anna, who would become a psychotherapist in her own right later in life, further analyzed her sister as someone who aims to enact all parts of a story to control the world around her, particularly a father whom she adores but who neglects her and also her mother, Edith. In Anna Campion's docudrama, *The Audition* (1989), she puts her sister's control on the big screen, to let us witness how Jane is directing her own elderly mother, who is asked to read and perform a poem. Edith, who is making many mistakes reading the poem, isn't let off the hook by daughter Jane, even when she repeatedly proclaims, "I can't do it." To which Jane responds, "Why don't we try it again from the beginning?"[55] Reversing power relationships can be helpful to work through psychic pain, as is known from the work of psychoanalyst Brett Kahr, quoted by Fox, who says that the meaning behind sexual fantasies can be explained with the "triumph of control."[56] In other words, according to Kahr, a sexual fantasy serves the purposes of controlling what is uncontrollable and providing psychic relief from the real pain, for instance, by switching positions with a perpetrator in the logic of the sexual fantasy:

> This kind of reversal is characteristic of any number of fantasies gathered through Kahr's research, in which an emotionally deprived woman seeks to reverse the real-life experience of an

> uninterested father by creating in her mind a man who has a compulsive interest in her and her body, and over whom she can take charge. To my mind, there is no doubt whatsoever that Campion's movie is presenting a fantasy of this sort.[57]

While I agree with this reading, I also think we need to look more closely at how Campion constructs this fantasy and what visual means she uses in the film as opposed to the novel. Dana Polan points out that the film's visual language centers on "a verbal battle of the sexes."[58] The DP for this film was Dion Beebe, a South African Australian cinematographer, who will go on to receive an Oscar for best cinematography for *Memoirs of a Geisha* (2005).[59] After Campion's collaboration with the English-born New Zealander Stuart Dryburgh in her previous three films, *An Angel at My Table* (1990), *The Piano* (1993), and *The Portrait of a Lady* (1996), Beebe worked with Campion for the first time shooting *Holy Smoke!* and will also become the cinematographer for *In the Cut* (2003). Visually, the "battle of the sexes" takes place in confined spaces within the Barron's home, and in the *Half Way Hut*, where PJ brings his patient and later lover Ruth to de-program her from her cult addiction. Ruth's original resistance to PJ, the family, and in general her life, is often shown against very strong color schemes in the blue and green range, expressing her interior world of confusion and oppression that I would also label a form of "feeling camera" enhanced by visual treatments and FX that I will discuss more below (Figures 18 and 19).

What is striking about this film, both in its cinematography and editing style, is the fact that it never lingers too long in one person's point of view. The confinement within this paradox, I would argue, is

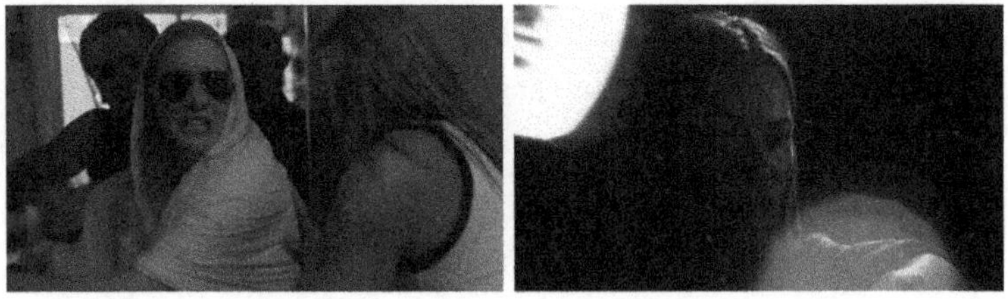

FIGURES 18 AND 19 Holy Smoke, *1999.*

presented as something that none of the characters can escape from. As a result, the film never asks to condemn PJ's abusive behavior of taking full advantage of his patient's fragility. As Dana Polan has it:

> No viewpoint is taken as final, no emotion or attitudes is endorsed as having unambiguous moral possession of truth and rightness. The editing style of cutting back and forth between characters sets up filmic spaces as one in which characters vie for domination but where the balance of power can be tipped back at any moment.[60]

I believe that the transgressive gaze in *Holy Smoke!* is very much construed out of the "film's undecidability of tone."[61] I suggest reading its resulting tonality of narrative sarcasm and visual hyperbole as a critique and mockery not necessarily just of the incest taboo in question and the reverse role-play of a sexual fantasy of controlling the father, but on a larger scale, of the theme of *appropriation*, and *power* as such: Westerners appropriating and consuming Eastern religious practices, men objectifying women, fathers abusing their power over their families. The story of *Holy Smoke!* shows that all of these abusive dynamics actually fail to make people happy, and as a result, the relationship between Ruth and PJ breaks apart in a dramatic denouement. During the final scenes, when PJ has actually understood his own faults and his own narcissism and begs for forgiveness, Ruth breaks up with him. PJ, now desperate, declares he wants to marry her. But Ruth has no interest in such a marriage and declines. Ruth and PJ now turn to what is left in them: physical violence, and start hitting one another. In his rage, PJ punches Ruth in the face. Ruth runs away with a bleeding jaw. Now comes the regret. PJ first follows Ruth in his car that paradoxically has antlers put on, and then runs after her through the vast and almost monstrous looking Australian Outer Banks that make him look even more like a desperate tiny little man. Dressed in a woman's dress, he is running after a young woman, who is drenched in blood. Just as the drama reaches its high point, we inhabit PJ's point of view which now again switches tone and turns into Screwball Comedy, where power shifts from scene to scene, and where the "screwball heroine" is often stronger than her male counterpart. Inhabiting PJ's delirious point of view, we now see Ruth merging into an iconic kitsch-image of a burning Indian-goddess-statue with six arms. This is not all that abruptly changes the tone of this scene from drama to satire. Ruth is now also waving her arms to the pop song playing under the scene, "Baby, It's You" (1969), by Burt Bacharach and Chrissie Hynde. In this pivotal end-sequence, the vibrant colors of gold, yellow, and orange have been enhanced digitally by the colors already in place in the scene but turned into a visual iconography of religious extasy.[62] Furthermore, a psychedelic pop-art vibe seems to be saying: any form of belief system or love-system is not only delusional but a form of consumption too (Figures 20–22).

While it would be worth to continue talking about the Gothic visual style of this unique film, I want to finish by returning to its important theme of transgression. PJ's "fairy-tale heroism," as Polan calls it, of saving and controlling the "fairy-princess" has turned dark and wild, diverging from the optimism of the traditional screwball comedy. Lovers and former mentor and mentee, PJ and Ruth, father Gilbert and daughter Ruth, Eastern and Western religions, can never overcome their differences. The epilogue shows a form of resignment and the collapse of all hopes for each of the characters: PJ has married Carol, his assistant, and is a father of twins, Ruth reveals she has a boyfriend and reports in a voice-over, "My Dad finally did run off with his secretary," which can be read as a reflection of Jane and Anna's parents' actual divorce that happened in real life. The ending, in other words, is completely disillusioning. All bubbles have popped. As Polan has it,

> this is the reverse of the tone of *The Piano*: where the earlier romantic film had ended with an affirmation of the couple interrupted by the reminder of the watery grave that might have been (and that continues to haunt Ada), *Holy Smoke* suggest that it

FIGURES 20, 21, AND 22 Holy Smoke! *1999.*

> is romance that might have been and that life is to be lived haunted by the regret at what was missed.[63]

There is an ambivalence in the relationship between fathers and daughters in Campion's films discussed thus far: from Pam in *A Girl's Own Story* to Lorraine being harassed by her boss John Phillips to Ruth in *Holy Smoke!* falling for PJ, the cult exit counselor. The difficulty, as Fox has already detected, is in a clear condemnation of the male offender. This theme will come back in full fledge with *In the Cut* and *The Power of the Dog*, which I will both discuss in Chapter 4.

The Transgressive Gaze

I want to summarize that Campion's early film period develops a "transgressive gaze" that exposes a woman's oppression from within the first "regime" that she is often subjected to: the family. Within this ecosystem, Campion's gaze presupposes the socially accepted mechanisms of heterosexuality and the "natural assumption of woman" that, as French feminist liberation movement co-founder Monique Wittig would have criticized, is presented as "natural" rather than "political."[64] In other words, for Wittig and many feminists from the women's liberation movement of the 1980s, the proposed escape route for this situation is the refusal of desiring men. But Campion's world is not that route. Rather, through the transgressive gaze, she shows a non-negotiable heterosexuality, which is represented with irony in the sequence from *A Girl's Own Story* of Pam and her girl entourage who are curiously learning about the biology of the erect phallus in a biology book, to Ruth's revolution and emancipation out of the Indian cult and then from PJ Waters, the "cult exiter" in *Holy Smoke!*. Lesbian desire isn't a part of Campion's early filmmaking's preoccupation, but she shows and puts on the screen the relentless world of the normatizing family, which is what her characters escape from. It isn't heterosexuality, but patriarchy itself. Campion's venture into the LGBTQ+ desire structure of her protagonists will change with *The Power of the Dog*.

Even though Campion's cinema is situated in a heteronormative world of women desiring men, I would argue for a reading of Campion's transgressive cinematic gaze as deeply political in that she shows how problematic and ill-constructed this "natural" domain of heterosexually socialized women is. Campion's authorial voice, to say it with Kaja Silverman, puts *women* behind the story, as authors and creators, as well as women in front of the camera as the "inhabitants" of this newly created world. As the psychoanalyst Jacqueline Rose has it: "For women especially, the supremest of autocrats is a father whose statue goes without question and beyond which there is no appeal. Feminism describes this structure as patriarchal."[65] In this sense, I disagree with Alistair Fox's overinterpretation of the "incestuous father-fantasy" present in Campion's oeuvre, but I see her emphasis on power structures and codependencies within the family fabric as groundwork in understanding the machinations of submission and power structures themselves. Campion is counteracting patriarchy in the sense of Rose by way of understanding its inner life. She puts her characters' and their inner and outer worlds on the screen not because she has a "social complaint," and as we know from her reaction to *After Hours*, she prefers not to be didactic with her cinema. Instead,

Campion's characters fail, they abandon each other, they hate each other, they are shown in their weaknesses, they remain unresolved, and yet she doesn't demand from us viewers to feel misery for them. In this regard, Campion's characters might be Nietzschean in the sense of *On the Genealogy of Morality* (1887), in which the philosopher criticizes the human emotion of sympathy, proclaimed by psychologists or by priesthood, and condemns those "self-proclaimed aristocrats" who think by saying they are better are being "good." In Campion's world, all that matters, just like for Nietzsche, is the *truth* of the character, or what Campion calls their authenticity: "I think that when we say authenticity what we mean is people applying themselves to understanding life. That's what attracted me to film in the first place."[66]

In Campion's early films, the marginalized, the yet-to-be-adults, or the never-to-be-adults such as Pam, Lorraine, Janet, Sweetie, and Ruth, appear normally socialized within the logic of their films because they are *authentic*. Thus, in the films discussed in this chapter, Campion's cinema is able to denature the idea of the "bad" by focusing on the outliers, the exceptions, the abnormal. There is an implicit idea about how the "good" is never a "natural quality" but hides in these sedimented power relations, and her characters act out against them even while not doing anything, because they have that Nietzschean "will to truth."

3

Women's Sexual Freedom

First Feature, and Mid-Career Features 1986–96

As announced in the introductory Chapter 1, in this chapter, I am dealing in depth with what I consider the central theme in Campion's philosophical film work: the condition of women's bodies, female sexuality at large, women inhabiting traditionally male workspaces, and women living out their sexual desires "like men." I will start with Campion's first feature film, *2 Friends* (1986), a film that tells the story of female adolescence and friendship among two girls that forms the basis for a happy female identity and sexuality. This film functions almost like an oracle for her later films discussed in this chapter, as when the girls drift apart, one of the girls also falls apart. I will then continue chronologically with *An Angel at My Table* (1990), a film that also fits the discussion of Campion's transgressive gaze from Chapter 2, in that it features a woman struggling with mental illness. However, I decided to include this film in Chapter 3's discussion of female self-determination, as, in the end, *An Angel at My Table* is predominantly a portrait and celebration of a woman making it in a man's world as she becomes a successful writer and fulfills her very own life dreams including her sexual desires. The core of this chapter, however, will be the discussion of two of the films that Campion has become most known for before her Oscar-winning *The Power of the Dog* (2021): *The Piano* (1993) and *The Portrait of a Lady* (1996). In my discussion of these two key films, I will continue from what Dana Polan has called the "deep emotionalism of *The Piano*" (with the central character of Ada) and the "intellectual coldness of *The Portrait of a Lady*" (with the central character of Isabel), and demonstrating how sexual liberation and sexual fantasies at large play the key role in the character arcs of both Ada and Isabel. I will also read and contextualize these films as critical forerunners to what I would call "recent feminist revisionary films" that have imagined historical female characters with a sexual drive *ante litteram*, as for instance Céline Sciamma's *Portrait of a Lady on Fire* (2019) or Marie Kreutzer's *Corsage* (2022).

The feminist philosopher Jacqueline Rose resists to understand women's sexuality from either a biological pre-given or a sociological role, as she points out with an understandable resentment that these positions "have in common the image of utter passivity they produce: the woman receives her natural destiny or else is marked over by an equally ineluctable social world."[1] I fully agree with Rose's skepticism toward the status quo of passivity in regards to the representation of female sexuality and self-awareness on-screen. To say it with Rose: any engagement with the image is driven by political intention. Most of the films that went beyond the classic "women-to-be-looked-at-ness" approach to femininity on-screen in the sense of Laura Mulvey's 1975 famous critique of the Hollywood era of the 1950s and 1960s,[2] could not evade a certain fundamentalism in terms of women's sexualized bodies on-screen, which Rose analyzes in three independent auteur films that were strongly influenced by the classic Hollywood tradition and came out between the years 1976–1978 (*Carrie*, *Coma*, and *Fedora*):

> Each film produces a self-consciousness of cinema, a kind of commentary on the very apparatus of the film, but then this very self-consciousness is reduced to the question of the body of the woman, of what is at stake in constituting her as the object (and subject) of the look.[3]

All of the female lead characters in these films, as Rose points out, are taken by a form of paranoia. However, rather than driving the storylines themselves, these women are investigated and looked at about their status quo of *woman* and, as I might add, they are not *speaking* woman, nor are they giving us an embodied female perspective at all. In other words, *Carrie*, *Coma*, and *Fedora* are putting the narrative emphasis on the investigation of femininity, which I believe derives directly as an extended gaze from their male directors (Brian de Palma, Michael Crichton, Billy Wilder) and the male authors that two of the stories are based on (Stephen King, Robin Cook). In Campion's films discussed in this chapter, on the other hand, femininity and female sexuality *drive* the stories themselves. A woman's sexual drive exists as a theme in these lead characters from the get-go and occurs in filmic storytelling and action, while our sexually active women characters either become or are fully aware of their sexual drives (even if they are repressed). I would, therefore, call Campion's films from her mid-career as truly turning the pages in cinema's feminist history and giving the new independent wave of narratives a true feminist face, one that it did not have before.[4] Thirty years before Sciamma's *Portrait of a Lady on Fire*, Campion's sexually aware feminist cinema arises in which the driving agent of the narratives is women's desires for (sexual) self-fulfillments themselves, as in the case of Janet (*An Angel at My Table*), Ada (*The Piano*), and Isabel (*The Portrait of a Lady*).

According to Christian Metz (*Film Language: A Semiotics of the Cinema*, 1974), the cinematic apparatus is more capable of grasping the spectator and taking them along on the ride of a subjective experience than any other representational arts: "I know that what I am seeing is not real but I will pretend whilst I am here that it is."[5] Rose seconds Metz's privileged reading of cinema as the "most imaginary" of representational apparatuses. What connects Metz and Rose's semiotics of cinema with Jane Campion's work is the fact that both the female lead characters represented on the screen and the viewer following their actions require an active engagement and a certain form of activism. This loop comes to full fruition with what I'd like to call a cinematic feminism that can be found in Campion's oeuvre from these years. This is a feminism that is no longer concerned with the question of looking *at* the woman but with the question of speaking from within femininity and hereby creating a unique genre that often blends tragic melodrama with romantic wish-fulfillment fantasy, which reminds us of the narrative style of the Brontë sisters in their novels.[6]

2 Friends, 1986

In Campion's first feature, *2 Friends*, Kelly and Louise are best friends. The end of the film, which is the beginning of their relationship, as the film is told in fragments and in reverse chronological order, shows their lives truly mirroring one another. But at the beginning of the film, we actually are thrown into the end of their relationship. After 13.5 minutes of a rather lengthy and a bit disorienting introduction to the film's characters, Louise, a proper looking student dressed in uniform, receives a reconciliation letter from her friend Kelly, which is waiting for her on her piano. While Kelly, who has been introduced on-screen as a punk with a mohawk, huge earrings, and a funky boyfriend, is buying a vase in a store, Louise opens the letter, and we hear it being read out loud through Kelly's voice-over. We immediately know that there has been a falling out of the two friends, and we will only later understand that Louise's indecision about accepting Kelly's apology letter was the "chronological endpoint of the narrative."[7] Throughout the film, we will get to know what drew these two friends apart through flashbacks up until the very innocent days of their carefree childhood. The narrative double-structure of the two friends, who are also the two main characters, is a foreshadow of the sister characters Sweetie and Kay in *Sweetie* (1989), discussed in the previous chapter, and of Frannie and Pauline in *In the Cut* (2003), discussed in Chapter 4. The two friends in *2 Friends* share a profoundly dysfunctional family background with each other and with so many of the Campion characters we know thus far from *A Girl's Own Story*, *After Hours*, and *Sweetie*. To compensate or escape from a disturbed family romance, the characters engage in a fantasy of incest, to continue Fox's psychoanalytic interpretation. Louise asks her father, with whom she is eating out at a restaurant, if he thinks that people might perceive them as a couple rather than as father and daughter: "Dad, do you think anyone would mistake us for boyfriend and girlfriend?" Kelly, on the other hand, makes the mistake of trusting her father's friend, who will take advantage of her. Both young girls' stories can be read as the attempt at finding adulthood by straightening out and removing themselves from their family backgrounds.

Let me start with Louise: the girl's dysfunctional background is only alluded to by the occasionally fighting parents. Eventually, the parents will split up, which is told implicitly in the film. Louise manages to develop into normal adulthood, while Kelly, despite the similar predispositions, falls through the cracks of society and falls victim to drugs, adulterous sex, and abuse. Just like Sweetie in *Sweetie*, Kelly in *2 Friends* seems not made for this world, and the world is surely not making it easy on her. Let me continue with Kelly, who is the main heroine of *2 Friends*: she is the child of a financially struggling working-class family and also the daughter of her parent's previous broken marriage. Her separated mother has remarried an abusive man, Malcolm, whom Kelly hates. Her mother, just like the mother character from *After Hours*, doesn't stand by her daughter but chooses her husband over her daughter. As a result, Kelly decides to live with her real father, whom she adores just like Louise does hers.

As mentioned earlier, the narrative structure of this film is inverted, and as we progress in the timeline of the film, we start understanding every step of the decisions that led to Kelly's downfall. The first big disturbance in Kelly's life occurs when her mother and stepfather prohibit her from joining her best friend, Louise, in attending the prestigious private high school, where both girls were admitted despite a very difficult admission test. This decision is driven by the stepfather Malcolm, who aggressively pronounces to the family that they would have to spend too much on Kelly's school, adding that he doesn't believe in higher education anyway. The other, even more dramatic disturbance and reason for Kelly's life falling to pieces, is when she becomes the victim of a domestic abuse situation. This key scene is told brilliantly in the film through color scheme and atmosphere changes, and no clear narrative explanation of what actually happened (i.e., we don't see any sexuality on the screen), mirroring the assault victim's perception and her trauma of repression. In this ambiguously told scene of a sexual assault, a friend of Kelly's father, a man in his forties, is called to "babysit" Kelly last minute, as her stepfather reports to him by phone that he needs to go out for an unforeseen "hot date." At first, Kelly and the man play harmless board games together, as if they were a harmonious father and daughter duo, but slowly the atmosphere changes from an innocent game night to some strange erotic tensions building between them (see Figure 23). This includes a particularly long take, a technique that is employed systematically in the film, which contributes to the tension bursting and breaking the "narrative flow into a series of self-sufficient tableaux."[8] As Polan reminds us, already in her earlier films, Campion engaged in the long take allowing the "resonant psycho-social situations to play themselves out."[9] When Kelly steps into her "babysitter's" room during the night worried if her father had come back yet, she unexpectedly lies down next to the man, as if his little child. Her move is supposed to feel ambiguous to the viewer: Is she looking for a protective father figure?

FIGURE 23 ***2 Friends**, 1986.*

Does she want something from the "babysitter"? We don't know. But we do know that when the "babysitter" suddenly abuses the proximity of the teenager in his bedroom and starts initiating sex with Kelly, she has a bad reaction. The shocked teenager leaves the room abruptly and in confusion, and while we did not see what exactly happened, we understand that she did not consent to it. It now starts to make sense to us that Kelly became a rebellious punk who uses bad language and smokes pot when thinking back at the first time we met her at the beginning of the film.

After the assault scene, the color scheme and scale of the film changes tonality. We are no longer in the room with our protagonists, but we see Kelly from above as a little figure walking away from her father's apartment in the middle of the night, giving us a sense of strange undefined danger (see Figure 24). A young girl wandering the streets, Kelly looks completely lost, and her human size has been scaled to the street signs and a traffic light that is ambiguously showing a green and red light at the same time. In this bluish-ice-cold-night

FIGURE 24 *2* **Friends,** *1986.*

atmosphere, we don't feel any emotionality of the character, whose face has been removed from our point of reference. For me, the small figure is an indication that the *2 Friends* have slipped apart. Kelly is on her own after this terrible event, and her former friend Louise doesn't even know what she is going through. While the film focuses on the potential of friendship and its failures, it also shows us that sex and, in particular, men with a sex drive are problems for girls. Overall, the two friends in *2 Friends* live in a world of dangers and are surrounded by careless incestuous father figures. "It is because of these awful men that a young woman like Kelly cannot develop into stable adulthood and a happy female sexual identity," the film is saying. While *A Girl's Own Story*, a film Campion made just two years earlier, stylized and celebrated the transgressive drives in a "girls' own world" per se, *2 Friends* showcases the negative effects of transgression from within the domestic environment. In some ways, with this sad story of a young woman not making it, *2 Friends* is preparing us for the world of *Sweetie* (1989), already discussed in Chapter 2. However, in *Sweetie*, the magic realist and absurdist treatment of Sweetie lets the character succeed *despite* her isolation, and even her death, which is staged like a celebration at the end of the film to the song "Love Me With All Your Heart." What is clear is that all three of these films deal with the same pressing question: Why do young girls have to fail?

Just like *Sweetie*, *2 Friends*, however, does not end on a negative note, but at the very end Campion introduces a new and unexpected storytelling device: animation and strong colorization techniques suddenly hybridize the film's tone and turn it into what Laura Mulvey has called a "woman-inflected modality of storytelling."[10] In such a kind of cinema, mixed media are used to create a multiplicity of meaning, referencing the instability and the continuum of the female identity. The end-sequence in *2 Friends* does exactly that: it introduces a new way of storytelling that the film hasn't seen thus far, mixing storytelling devices, which also creates a humorous relief: like in the depiction of young women's school uniforms and their matching socks and shoes, one of Campion's screen favorites, in this animated shot the bare girls' legs have been penciled over or crossed out in brown and red (Figure 25).

To say it with Gwendolyn Audrey Foster,

> in the film's final heartbreaking moments, the film bursts into a Richard Lester-style segment of visual extravagance, using stop motion, mattes, vibrant hand coloring, and other special effects to suggest the beauty and joy of young Kelly and Louise's early friendship, as they pledge undying friendship, draft a letter to the local newspaper decrying the proliferation of nuclear weapons,

FIGURE 25 *2* Friends, *1986.*

and seem destined for a life of female solidarity and success. And it's on this hopeful note that the film ends.[11]

However, I want to add that the inverted narrative structure prevents us from feeling ever 100 percent positively about the characters, since we have known their fate from the very beginning of the film, one a drug addict and one a seemingly unloyal friend. While it is acutely painful to witness this ending at the very beginning, there is also something deeply satisfying about seeing an uncomfortable truth about young women's lack of place in society so plainly stated.

2 Friends was shot by Australian cinematographer Sally Bongers who had already shot Campion's acclaimed short *Peel* discussed in Chapter 1. As Michel Ciment has it, its unique style showed "signs of the shooting style of Antonioni—particularly of *Le Amiche* (1955)—with its long sequence shots, depths of field, ellipses, and a liking for the unsaid and empty shots."[12]

2 Friends is the first of several of Campion's films, which is based on a novel or a screenplay not authored by Campion but turned into her own authorship and her own intrinsic film language. While the film is based on a script by the Australian novelist Helen Garner, who also gave it its inverted narrative structure, it clearly "foreshadows the authoring strategy that Campion would use again in converting Henry James's novel *The Portrait of a Lady* and Susanna Moore's novel *In the Cut* into films that are fully transformed into her personal cinema."[13] *2 Friends* is also the first film for which Campion had been approached by the producer of many of her future films, Jan Chapman, and was commissioned for Australian television release. Chapman and Campion's collaboration will culminate in *The Piano*, which I am discussing further below. For now, I am remaining within the chronology of Campion's film productions with the next film, also commissioned for Australian television and also based on a novel that wasn't authored by Campion herself, that is, the famous autobiographical writings of the celebrated New Zealand author Janet Frame.

An Angel at My Table, 1990

It is time to look in-depth at Campion's mid-career films, *An Angel at My Table*, *The Piano*, and *The Portrait of a Lady*. Alistair Fox described these three films as belonging to one group of films that are dealing with the "psychodynamics involved in the condition of women who are depressed or repressed."[14] I would like to expand on Fox's psychoanalytic reading and think of these films as investigations of depressed and repressed women's bodies in the first place, and of depressed and repressed women only in the second place. Each of these films is an exploration of a woman's desire for independence (from the parents, from a husband, from patriarchy at large), and each of them shows the character both failing and succeeding. Unlike today's recent wave of feminist empowerment films, from the historical drama *Portrait of a Lady on Fire* (2019) to the blockbuster *Barbie* (2023), Campion's mid-career heroines are not empowered—yet. In fact, they are trapped inside a patriarchal, societal, socio-economic, or historical structure that they seem to not be able to escape from. Because they have never lived independently or know the world outside of that structure, they are lacking the language of how to act freely. What they don't lack, however, is the *desire* to be freed, and the passion to inhabit and own their own bodies and realize their own sexual liberation. Unlike her previous work, these mid-career films are serious business, so to speak, and while they also show the Campion usual humor, they change and adapt the film languages to a more serious tone. More than that, they also stand on the shoulders of Campion's first feature film, which showed a young woman's desire for independence but ended up highlighting the societal traps and the character's failures. In *2 Friends*, Louise and Kelly had the same conditions to become successful young women, but one of them did not make it. A 50 percent negative outcome. In the following, I want to highlight the condition of women's bodies in each of these mid-career films to understand how the status quo of their bodies influences the heroines' professional and personal developments, what makes them fail and what makes them succeed.

Janet Frame, the main character of *An Angel at My Table*, is one single protagonist, as opposed to several protagonists in many of her films, which have a dual set of sisters or friends as main characters (*2 Friends, Sweetie,* or *In the Cut*) a "doubling motive" that shows Campion's interest in merging various characters' traits into one human psyche. Janet grows up in a working-class family in the South of New Zealand. Her parents, of Scottish descent, have five children; one of Janet's siblings dies in an accident, and another one suffers from epileptic seizures. The father works for the New Zealand railway, and the mother works as a housemaid in a writer's home. Janet struggles with mental illness, which leads her to having to be incarcerated in a psychiatric asylum for alleged schizophrenia. The stay in the psychiatric ward, which includes electroshock treatments, is traumatizing for Janet. She is scheduled for a lobotomy, which fortunately she does not have to undergo by a hair, as it gets canceled last minute. Against all the odds, Janet manages to become a successful poet and author. This deeply feminist film peels back in two and a half hours what it takes to survive in a world that isn't made for women, does not care about women, nor has any understanding of their struggles, especially the tabooed issue around mental illness. As Polan has it, "the film chronicles the needs of its heroine to be free of all direction by the will of other people, including that of men as sexual partners."[15]

The film is based on Janet Frame's famous autobiography, by the homonymous title *An Angel at My Table* (1984). The title itself is a quote from one of Rainer Maria Rilke's fifty-nine poems from the *Vergers* (Orchards) collection, which he wrote between 1924 and 1925 in the French language and which were published in 1926, the year of his death. As is well-known, Rilke struggled with mental illness himself and was hospitalized in a sanatorium in Montreux, Switzerland, toward the end of his life. Janet Frame quotes the poem at the beginning of part two of her autobiography in the French original to allude to the "angel of madness" that might, one day, choose one's table. I want to include it here in its English translation:

> Stay still, if suddenly
> the Angel chooses your table:
> softly smooth the wrinkles
> in the cloth beneath your bread.[16]

Campion's filmic adaptation, which was written by Laura Jones but was heavily edited by Campion, is structured like the autobiography itself, in three parts. The first part is called *To the Is-land*, and deals with Janet's childhood. It is told episodically in a series of fragments, which also allows for the use of three different actresses without any narrative disruption, focusing on the development of her character during her youth. There are many little stories told in a classic Campionesque theatrical fashion, from the infamous gum story, where Janet offers gum to her classmates, which she has bought with the money she stole from her father, and for which she gets punished—to several performance episodes (school auditions, plays, neighbor dances, etc.). The first part shares indeed a certain familiarity with *Sweetie* in its farcical depiction of Janet's life among so many siblings and in an impoverished chaotic household. The casting is great, and the fact that each of the actresses is wearing the same red-haired wig helps to connect the characters easily. The second part is titled after the film itself, *An Angel at My Table*, and deals with Janet's mental illness and her more pronounced episodes of anxiety. It starts with Janet leaving home to start living with her Aunty Isy and Uncle George and attending Dunedin Training College, where she is educated as a school teacher, but after six weeks of college, she is diagnosed with schizophrenia. This middle part changes in tone to a serious narrative, one that we haven't seen in a Campion film before, culminating in Janet's hospitalization at Dunedin Public Hospital's psychiatric ward and, after an unsuccessful suicide attempt, her referral to Seacliff asylum. This and the third part are filmed with a certain visual sobriety, which Campion explained with the fact that she did not want to take away from Janet's story through a too anesthetized film language. The third part, *The Envoy from Mirror City*, alludes to Janet's inner life as a writer and her force of imagination which saves her during the time of her hospitalizations. She writes her first novel on that very same theme of mental illness, *Owls Do Cry* (1957), while living in Takapuna in a shack on the property of the whimsical writer Frank Sargeson who never wears a shirt; part three continues through her travels overseas and leaving New Zealand for a total of seven years—to Paris, London, Ibiza, and Andorra, where she is sent with a prestigious literary scholarship after having her first novel published to acclaim.

While the film is inspired and based on the book's three-part structure, Campion gives it her own very personal stamp, picking out only the episodes from a total of nearly 600 pages that are relevant to either her or her mother Edith's story, which became the basis of her adaptation. To say it with Alistair Fox, *An Angel at My Table* is Campion's full-on "mother film," as it is inspired and based on Edith Campion's mental illness, her suicide attempts, and many of the episodes described in the film happened in Edith's real life. But as we also know from many interviews Campion has given on this film, the adaptation is also woven in with her own biography, as Campion used many elements from her own childhood memory, such as her fear of getting her first period, to just give one of many examples, and melds them in with Frame's and her mom's. Edith Campion, Jane's own mother, becomes an actual character in *An Angel at My Table's* first part, where she is playing the short but memorable performance of Janet's poetry teacher, Miss Lindsay, who is reciting in an exalted fashion Tennyson's *Idylls of the King* (Figures 26–28). The pupils, and especially Janet, are fascinated by the teacher, as can be seen from the reverse shot (Figure 29) of young Janet's entranced face blown up to full screen, which also accounts for a certain comic relief.

Edith's cameo early in the film is more of a gimmick as the mother character, Lottie, who had a prominent role in the book as a poet in her

FIGURES 26, 27, AND 28 An Angel at My *Table, 1990.*

FIGURE 29 An Angel at My *Table, 1990.*

own right, is actually downplayed in the adaptation, and Campion's focus on the parents is clearly on Janet's father, whom I will return to later on in more detail.

Let me digress about mother figures in Campion's films here. Mothers are either absent, powerless, or indeed betraying their children in all of Campion's films. In *Peel*, the mother was in fact missing entirely on the family road trip; in *A Girl's Own Story*, the mother was there but mute (as will be the case for Ada in *The Piano*); in *After Hours*, the mother betrayed her daughter; in *Sweetie*, the mother is irresponsible; in *2 Friends*, the mothers are powerless, living under the spell of their husbands. As Fox points out, in *In the Cut*, discussed in Chapter 4, we get the impression that the mother is dead through the main character Frannie's fantasy recollection.[17] Campion has stated publicly that she had a controversial relationship with her mother Edith. In an interview with Sue Williams during the production of *An Angel at My Table*, she talks openly about her mother suffering from depression and having to be hospitalized for this disease.[18] Campion's desire to weave her actual mother into her film has been captured on camera by her sister Anna in her acclaimed documentary film *The Audition*, 1989. The film, which I mentioned already in Chapter 2, follows Jane and Edith on a drive to their home in Otaki, New Zealand, where Edith rehearses the part of Miss Lindsay for her daughter, the director. The fricative interaction between Jane and her mother in *The Audition* has been discussed widely, as it openly reveals their complex relationship in eternity, captured on film. In this domestic ethnography, sister Anna Campion observes the interaction between her sister, the film auteur, and their mother, interviewed by Jane. When Edith talks about waking up each morning with a fear of her marriage failing, which later on happens in real life, Jane, listening behind the camera, takes a breath from an inhaler. The inclusion of this gesture in *The Audition* is a literal allusion to Edith suffering from asthma as a child. What is more, it also implies that "mother and daughter are alike rather than having separate personalities,"[19] another duality in Campion's characters. Thus, *The Audition* is a film that exposes the real relationship between Jane and Edith in a way that one could compare to a reality television drama, as the director pushes the protagonist visibly to do something they don't really want or that they fear. Campion's insistence to put her mother in *An Angel at My Table*, the autobiographical adaptation of the poet Janet Frame's life story, is a clear indication that the mother's bodily presence means a lot and isn't just a *representation*. In the authorial hands of Jane, Edith is made to become Janet, who is also Jane.

> Throughout the film, the tension between Edith and Jane is palpable. It becomes clear that Edith has serious doubts about taking the role—she says several times that she does not actually want to do it, that someone better could be found. Yet Jane, on the other hand, repeatedly insists that she is perfect for it, and that if she took the part it "would mean a lot" to her. In the film's final scene, Edith performs a monologue from her past acting career, and as she finishes, tears appear in Jane's eyes.[20]

I agree with Alexis Brown in the conclusion of the reading of *An Angel at My Table* that by merging the lived experiences of the author Janet Frame with her mother's and her own, Campion gained authorial control over a biography that wasn't hers but that she invested her own very personal childhood memories in, and that could have become hers. I would even go as far as to say she feared that it could become hers in that she was well aware that mental illness is also a hereditary illness. In other words, gaining control over Janet Frame's story was also a way to control her mom's illness, and eventually maintaining her own sanity.[21] Or to say it with Fox in a more explicitly psychoanalytic reading, referencing the fact that Campion remembers to have cried hard, while reading Frame's first part of the autobiography for the first time:

> The weeping that was triggered in Jane as a response to *To the Is-Land* shows Jane identifying with Janet as if she (both Jane and Janet) were Jane's mother, Edith—which suggests a mirroring in Jane's own life of her other's unhappiness, which she is moved to act out as a result of intense empathic identification. [. . .] look at it from one perspective and one will see Edith in Janet; slightly change the angle from which it is viewed, and one will see Jane in Janet.[22]

This empathetic identification helps Campion to make mental illness the powerful engine of the film. The illness is the source not only for Janet Frame's anxiety and mental illness but also for her eventual success as an author. In other words, Campion turns her character's illness into something positive. While this is not yet the spirit of the "empowerment films" from today's feminist era, we don't encounter Janet Frame's illness as something entirely negative or hopeless, as there is always a sense of humor and optimism in the filmic representation of Janet's psyche. Interestingly, while Campion admits that she herself had inclinations toward depression, she also reiterates she is fundamentally an optimist.[23] For instance, in part three, while living in Spain with her scholarship, Janet experiences her first big love affair with Bernhard, a visiting American history professor and writer from the United States. This love affair results in a pregnancy and then in a miscarriage. Bernhard is shown as a narcissistic jokester man whom we, in fact, never even properly see in a full frame, that's how "unimportant" he seems to Campion's storyline. Campion tells the story of Janet's miscarriage in London as an abortion that luckily expunges any traces of Janet's sexual encounter with this man. What is more, Campion puts her actual mother's story into the storyline of Janet and Bernhard's loss of a baby. In real life, Edith lost a baby boy in London in 1949 to a miscarriage, and almost in an uncanny foreshadowing of her own life, Jane Campion will lose her baby boy in 1993 to a miscarriage after finishing *The Piano*.

Bernhard is not the only non-committed man aligning himself with the theme of passive bystanders, or worse, people actively betraying each other, a theme threading itself through all films of Jane Campion. Let's not forget part II of *An Angel at My Table*, where there is also the professor, who Janet has a crush on, but who betrays her by having her hospitalized. While I do not have the space to include a more thorough discussion of *An Angel at My Table* here, I want to end on one key point: the positively portrayed role of Janet Frame's father, Curly, who helps and assists his daughter Janet in achieving her success, unlike many of the unreliable fathers we have seen so far in her films, who were unfaithful, irresponsible, and absent. In an act of symbolic appropriation of manhood, at the very end of the film, Janet steps into her father's shoes, after he has already passed away. This scene wasn't included in the autobiography by Janet Frame and only appeared in a minor form in Laura Jones's screenplay. Campion changed it and made it into a big visual and narrative statement: stepping into the father's manly shoes becomes the predisposition for a successful life.

This image of a woman in men's shoes also reminds us of the feminist short *The Lady Bug* (2007), which I have described in Chapter 1, where a woman is being smushed by the man's shoes (Figure 30).

To go back to the introduction of this chapter and in reference to Jacqueline Rose's emphasis on the engagement with the image as belonging to a political intention, it is interesting to note that *An Angel at My Table* is not driven by a woman's sexual or erotic self-awareness like the two pivotal films discussed subsequently in this chapter. In fact, there is little eroticism in An Angel. To say it with Polan:

> If *The Piano* presents a woman learning to grow by transferring her affection from an instrument of art to other people, *An Angel at My Table* offers an alternate feminine narrative, one about self-sufficiency, one about art as a salvation from the ravages of the social.[24]

Instead, the maturation of the character into a fully grown-up independent woman occurs through an imaginative transformation

FIGURE 30 An Angel at My *Table, 1990.*

which takes place through writing—from a passive observer and a figure of solitude to a successful writer who assumes control of her own creative life.[25] While a lived sexuality does not play a key role, I want to conclude this discussion by remembering the last shot in the film. As many film critics before me have pointed out, in this shot, Janet turns herself into the object of voyeurism. No longer is she the one looking at others (most notably her sister Myrtle, who she looks at as she goes off to the baths where she will drown), but "a figure to be looked at with respect and admiration."[26]

The Piano, 1993

While *An Angel at My Table* was the first New Zealand film ever shown at the Venice Film Festival, where it won the Silver Lion and Grand Jury prizes, and additionally the Australian Film Critics' Circle awarded it the prize for Best Foreign Film, Campion's next film, *The Piano*, brought her not only many more prizes but world fame and fandom. As I already summarized in Chapter 1, *The Piano*, which was produced by Jan Chapman, won the main prize of the Palme d'Or at the Cannes Film Festival in 1993, making Campion the first female director to receive this award. In 1994, it also won three Academy Awards out of eight total nominations for "Best Actress" (Holly Hunter in the main role of Ada), "Best Supporting Actress" (Anna Paquin in the role of Ada's daughter Flora), and "Best Original Screenplay" for Jane Campion. In *The Piano*, we occupy the perspective of mute Ada McGrath, a mid-nineteenth-century pianist from Scotland who has arrived in New Zealand with her young daughter and her piano.

Ada, who hasn't spoken since a traumatic event happened in her childhood, was sold by her father into marriage to a New Zealand frontiersman called Alisdair Stewart (played by Sam Neill). Ada can only communicate through sign language and with the help of her nine-year-old daughter Flora. In her new home, Ada falls in love with a retired sailor who has taken on Maori customs, by the name of George Baines, and legendarily played by Harvey Keitel. Baines, too, falls in love with Ada, who gives him piano lessons. Over time the lessons turn into a passionate love relationship initiated by Baines. When her husband Alisdair Stewart finds out about the adultery from her daughter Flora, he doesn't first react but then suddenly punishes Ada in a brutal act of mutilation by cutting off of her middle finger with an ax. Ada cannot play the piano anymore, but this event leads her to leave Stewart and to travel back to Scotland together with George Baines. During the crossing of the ocean, Ada drowns the piano, considering drowning with it but then decides to stay alive. Once back in Scotland, she is shown to build a happy family life with George and Flora.[27]

Before going into detail about the film's visual language and themes, I want to start by pointing out the unique cult effect of this film, without which we would certainly be cutting short and totally diminishing *The Piano*'s overall success outside of the box office and critical acclaim. In his book about Campion that has heavily informed my own research, Dana Polan dedicates a whole early chapter just to the "phenomenon" of the film, as it divided and shaped Campion's career in a way that will be unrepeated until *The Power of the Dog*'s success in 2021, which I will describe in Chapter 4. In other words, there is the Campion before and after *The Piano*. This phenomenon cannot be better described than with traditional cult and fandom reactions, which were provoked by the bonding experiences that the film evoked among its especially female viewers. In fact, I myself remember a rather shy and introverted colleague at Vienna University who told me about watching *The Piano*, when it had just come out in 1993. She talked about the film with glowing eyes and the biggest smile I had ever seen on her face. It seemed almost as if she had entered a sect or cult after this experience.

> Many women, in particular, attest to a profound intense bonding with *The Piano*, a strong sense of connection in which the effusive affect of the relationship of spectator to screen is insisted on. [. . .] "I fell into a sea of emotions that I hadn't discovered." [. . .] "It touched me deeply and I'm obsessed with it." [. . .] "is the best movie I have ever seen." [. . .] "I have seen it 94 times."[28]

The American film and media theorist Vivian Sobchack reports that when she watched *The Piano*, she was so intensely concentrated on the world on-screen that she felt catapulted to a "heightened instance of her common sensuous experience," feeling as if she was touched by the substance and texture of the images, particularly through the opening sequence. She describes this strong emotional impact and a crude bodily response on her senses, especially after watching the two opening shots (Figures 31 and 32), in an interesting form of self-ethnography as a viewer:

> In particular, I want to examine my sensual and sense-making experience of *The Piano*'s inaugural two shots. Although my body's attention was mobilized and concentrated throughout a film that never ceased to move or touch me in the most complex and various ways, these first two shots, at least to me, foreground the issue "at

> hand" (so to speak) in our engagement not only with this film, but to varying degree, with all others.
>
> Despite my "almost blindness," the "unrecognizable blur," the resistance of the image to my eyes, *my fingers knew what I was looking at*—and this in advance of the objective "reverse" shot that followed and put those fingers in their "proper" place (that is, where they could be objectively seen rather than subjectively looked through). What I was seeing was, in fact, from the beginning, *not* an unrecognizable image, however blurred and indeterminate in my vision, however much my eyes could not "make it out." From the first (although I didn't "know" it until the second), my fingers *comprehended* that image, *grasped* it with a nearly imperceptible tingle of attention and anticipation and, off-screen, "felt themselves" as a potentiality in the subjective situation figured on-screen. And this before I *re-cognized* my carnal comprehension into the conscious thought: "Ah, those are fingers I am looking at."[29]

Ada's body doesn't appear on the screen in a conventional or recognizable way at the beginning of *The Piano*. As Vivian Sobchack has it, we feel Ada's fingers before entirely understanding what we see. These "liquid fingers" are followed immediately by a crystal-clear perspective, "as they become matter-of-fact-objects to the lens of the camera."[30] This famous opening sequence of a blurred subjective viewpoint followed by a close-up of Ada's face and hands looking at us through her fingers (a finger that will later be chopped off violently in an act of pure misogyny), is followed by several shots in a rural environment giving us a glimpse of Ada's figure through a softly moving dolly shot that starts from a tree, which Ada is seated against,

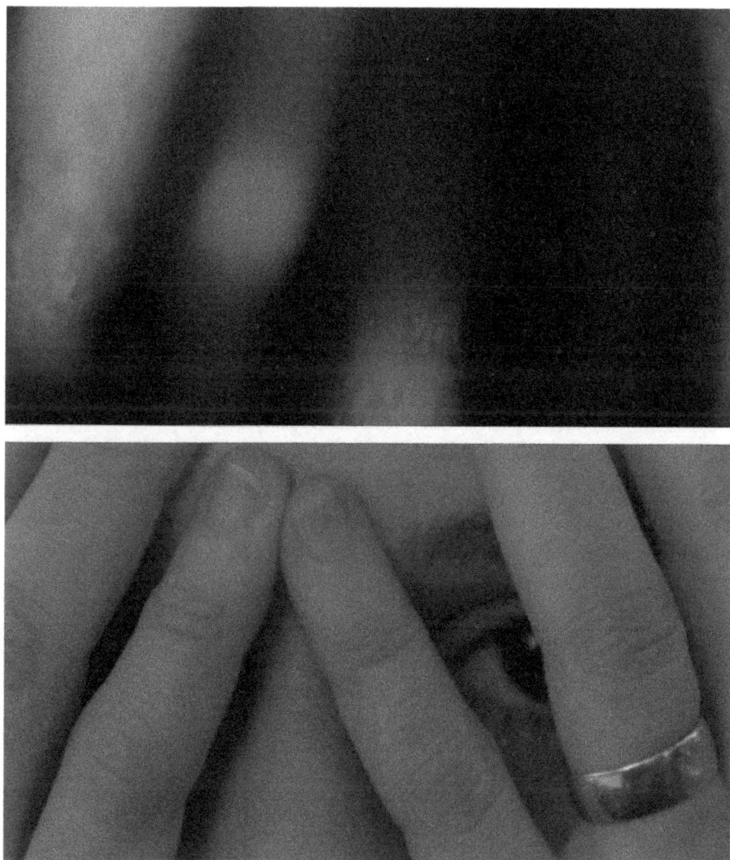

FIGURES 31 AND 32 **The Piano,** ***1993, opening shots.***

and from which the camera slowly swifts up into the sky. With this caressing camera motion, which has been equaled to "choreograph life as energy and uplift,"[31] we are introduced and invited to *feel* the screen and hence the world that Ada, the character, is embedded in before we can *understand* it or can place it geographically. What is more, the tentativeness of Ada's look at the camera and us, as shown in the above Figures 31 and 32, through her fingers, makes us—by which I mean us "women"—immediately into an accomplice on the heroine's journey. Indeed, Ada's look and her longing becomes our longing, as Dana Polan puts it in his close reading of three scenes of the film.

One of the scenes in question occurs early in the film, about fifteen minutes in, when upon their arrival in New Zealand, Ada is forced to leave her piano on the beach, as it is too heavy for the Maori people to carry up to the village where Ada, her daughter Flora, and her new husband Alisdair, whom they only just met, are supposed to start a life together. In this shot, Ada and Flora are looking from a cliff down at the piano, which is situated in the far distance with a sense of longing. But in the next moment, the group of Maori people continues and leaves the object of desire behind (Figure 33).

The "woman's film" that so many critics see represented in this pivotal Campion film, takes its origin in this narrative structure of longing and wish-fulfillment by a female character. It is a motive that will also return in Campion's next film, *The Portrait of a Lady*, in the figure of Gilbert Osmond promising Isabel Archer, Henry James's

FIGURE 33 The Piano, *1993*.

and Campion's main character, a wonderful life through marriage. In *The Piano,* the mythical wish expressed by Ada and realized through the film's visceral language is the actual object of the piano and not marriage. All of Ada's wishes are expressed through the piano. She wants to play it when she arrives in New Zealand but can't because it cannot be transported to her house. George Baines, played by Harvey Keitel, who had his breakthrough in Quentin Tarantino's *Reservoir Dogs* just a year before *The Piano* is portrayed as a male sex symbol by Campion, manages to get it into his house, and through the experience of giving him piano lessons, she eventually falls in love with him (notably after he sexually harasses her in a non-consensual way). The piano is hence the only vessel and way she can communicate to the world since she cannot speak. Through her fingers' touch, Ada can play it and "speak" to us; touch is also the sense that is being most strongly evoked by the camera work of DOP Stuart Dryburgh, who uses Campion's directive of an underwater feel for the film, also in the forest scenes and certainly in the romantic love scenes.

The Piano has been a popular object of Jungian analysis because of the archetypal realm of a woman's world it catapults the viewer into from the very opening of the blurred subjectivity to the very ending shots that take place underwater. The primordial element of water functions similarly to the element of fire in *Holy Smoke!* but another dimension is added in *The Piano*: the dimension not just of sexual freedom, the theme of her previous films, but of a woman's sexual satisfaction. But as Polan points out (and through the title of the *The Piano* chapter itself called "Dividing Lines") not all feminists saw this mythical film language and narrative of a muted woman finding satisfaction through a forbidden love with a "primitive man" in a positive light. The critique came mainly from the fact that Campion traded her previous genre of the melodrama for romance, and that *The Piano* was exposed and emphasized a woman's fixation, through the object of the piano, and that indeed her primary obsession was not the fundamental realization of her desire but rather the regressive and repressive manifestation of the very blockage of a free expression and true desire. In other words, Ada had to learn to break free from the piano, her obsession, and only through this clear demarcation can she become a subject in her own right. Yet, in *The Piano*'s storyline, she is never a fully independent subject, as after her escape from New Zealand and from her husband Alisdair Stewart, she will move in with a different man, George Baines, who has possessed her sexually, and whom she perhaps loves for the sake of hew own domination. While it is true that Ada's freedom as a woman and her sexual freedom are fully and 100 percent dependent on the men, absent or present, in her life, we also need to recognize that the story is anchored in a mid-nineteenth-century historical setting, and therefore bound to a commentary about that very time as a historical feature. One of the feminist defenders of Campion's *The Piano* is the psychoanalytic film critic Cynthia Kaufman, who interpreted Ada's resistance to language applying Kristeva's theories as a conscious decision to "not speaking the language of the father" and in consequence as the "ultimate act of resistance."[32] Jaime Bihlmeyer points out the connection between Kristeva's theoretical and Campion's cinematographical and narrative emphasis on the difficulty of a separation from the mother's body, which he explains from a technical psychoanalytic point of view:

> Campion concurs with Kristeva that the separation of the subject from the body-centered object is always already incomplete and that the source of the subject-in-process is the m/other.[33]

The separation from the mother is indeed also the framework chosen by Alistair Fox to read into *The Piano*'s deep structure. For Fox, after Campion had worked through her mother's depression in the adaptation of Janet Frame's biography, she was now ready to work on the question of the separation from the mother. No coincidence for Fox that *The Piano* is dedicated to Campion's mother Edith at the end of the film.

It took Campion six years to work on the screenplay for *The Piano*, called *The Piano Lesson* at first, which was loosely based on a 1920 New Zealand novel called *The Story of a New Zealand River* by Jane Mander. In this novel, an unwed Scottish woman called Alice who comes from a puritanical society, experiences a culture shock when she arrives in the Maori culture of colonial New Zealand, together with her vivacious, naïve nine-year old daughter. Just like Ada, the purpose of her trip is that Alice is forced to marry a man against her will and who she never met before for reasons of social propriety. In interviews, Campion said that she had the idea for this film already in 1984 after graduating from the Australian Film Television and Radio School, but it took her many years to make. She put it aside while making *Sweetie* and *An Angel at My Table*. Campion worked on the screenplay on her own, which she outlined with these opening sentences:

> New Zealand's first piano was left abandoned on a beach. Alice's husband could not see the use for it. However, Alice's attachment to her piano was unique, for she was mute.[34]

For Fox, it is precisely the attachment to the piano that represents the symbol of Ada's repressed passion and explains the archetypal quality of the film and its exploration of female desire. The piano is a symbol for the mother-child dyad from the early childhood and what is called the pre-mirror stage of the child not being able to separate their physical sense of the body from their mother's body. Of course, the visual emphasis on the underbelly through the poetic underwater imagery, shown in slow motion in the end-sequence, reflects on such a reading. Fox and the male psychoanalyst, O-Neill Dean, point out in their analytical reading:

> this process became arrested when the young Ada was six years old, leaving her "stuck" at an arrested stage of psychological development that is represented in the symbiotic mother-daughter-relationship between Ada and her daughter, Flora, with its extraordinary mirroring.[35]

Associative meaning can also be found in the figure of Bluebeard, and the fairytale that is put on in the film in the form of a shadow play, with young Flora on the stage and her proud mother Ada watching her perform. As Fox has pointed out, and as I have emphasized in Chapter 2, Campion's duals in the form of sisters, or in this case a mother and daughter, are there to show the different aspects of a self, splitting these characteristics up into two different people. While Flora is part of the play, it is really Ada who is seeing herself in this shadow play, in which Bluebeard kills his youngest wife as she has unveiled his secret, foreshadowing the violent act of Stewart chopping off Ada's finger: a finger we saw in the very opening shot as a blur and then a clear sharp image. This incident was based on Campion's autobiography which she shared in the Director's Commentary to *The Piano*:

> I went to one of these dances at a mental hospital. They had it in a gym. I can still remember this woman was there, and she'd chopped her gand off, her left hand off, because her husband was having an affair with someone, and she was trying to pull off her wedding ring, but it wouldn't come off, and in the heat of her desperation she went into the garage, got the axe, and hacked her hand off, and my mother was explaining this to me at the same time as we were watching her and her husband dancing at the dance in the gym. This is part of where I got the inspiration for the idea in *The Piano*, when Stewart chops Ada's finger off.[36]

While *An Angel at My Table* inscribed itself in a Gothic tradition of a woman caught in a malevolent space, *The Piano* explores issues of a woman's imprisonment by her gender, race, and historical condition in relation to the period of European colonization through the genre of the romance. Many film critics have analyzed the wildly romantic plot in the film, and Kathleen McHugh has even pointed out that Ada is a "composite of the attributes of the women artists who inspired Campion, combining Emily Brontë's silence, Emily Dickinson's secrecy, and Frida Kahlo's fierce gaze."[37]

The camerawork in *The Piano* emphasizes character development and not just classic epic cinema. While a lot of dolly shots were used, the camera operators followed their subjects' movements similar to a verité documentary style. Rather than just revealing the character by letting them move into a previously composed frame, they follow their actions. In that sense, the characters are determining the narrative by their actions (like in a documentary), and not the other way around. As Jane Campion herself explains:

> I wanted to photograph a story that has epic qualities without seeming a clone of David Lean (note: Lawrence of Arabia, Doctor Zhivago)—to still have my identity but also have a feminine epic quality and to recreate it so that the epicness didn't feel like it relates back to other big-look movies.[38]

There is no doubt but to interpret the choice of making the main character Ada a mute character as a strong feminist move for all the reasons already mentioned above. The character does not want to communicate, and as mentioned in the psychoanalytic reading by Kristeva, she refuses to speak the language of her forefathers, and of patriarchy, who traumatized her. Her secret love affair with George Baines and her refusal to speak make Ada all the more powerful. Campion herself clarifies that Ada has united the power of the secret with the power of the refusal to speak:

> I always saw her as someone who had removed herself very powerfully herself from life. She chose not to speak. It's never quote made clear why, and it appears even she can't remember the reason.[39]

In an interview about her role of Ada, Holly Hunter said that she felt both female and male forces in her character, which references this reunion of classic male strength with the stereotype of the female secret. This is why the character study of Ada reminds me of the more recent feminist historical film, *Portrait of a Lady on Fire*, which came out in a high time of gender fluidity and the LGBTQ+ movement.

The Piano, on the other hand, was made almost thirty years earlier and must therefore be seen as an absolute forerunner to this feminist revisionist genre, in which a woman in a historical time of repression, the nineteenth century, is portrayed as having not only a point of view of her own, but as having a sexual drive of her own. But *The Piano* is more than that. It is not only a film that critically investigates women's dependencies on men but also the colonized' dependencies on the colonizers and the lower classes' dependency on the upper class. In the end, the film shows that the emancipation from these ties is the only way to gain subjectivities. Quite literally, this is shown in the end-sequence that takes us into the underbelly of Ada's mind and into the deep ocean, where the film started: the crossing of the South Pacific Ocean from Scotland to New Zealand.

As Fox points out in reading Ada's suicidal fantasy to drown together with her piano, when Ada "places her foot in the coils of a rope tied to her piano, which has been thrown overboard, and thus allows herself to be drawn underwater into the depths of the sea."[40] But what is decisive about Ada's move is that she decides to let go of the cord, emancipating herself from the burden of the piano and from her ties to the past (Figure 34).

On the level of the sound, we experience a careful separation of the character's initial silence, which is broken through her inner voice, heard from the beginning on in her voice-over narration, and which is emphasized in Michael Nyman's beautiful original score, as well as the diegetic sound of the film—all of these auditory codes bring out the protagonist's search for a sense of self-expression and especially a new erotic self-awareness, as she finds herself in the unfamiliar place of colonial New Zealand. Campion, as in all her films, is mostly

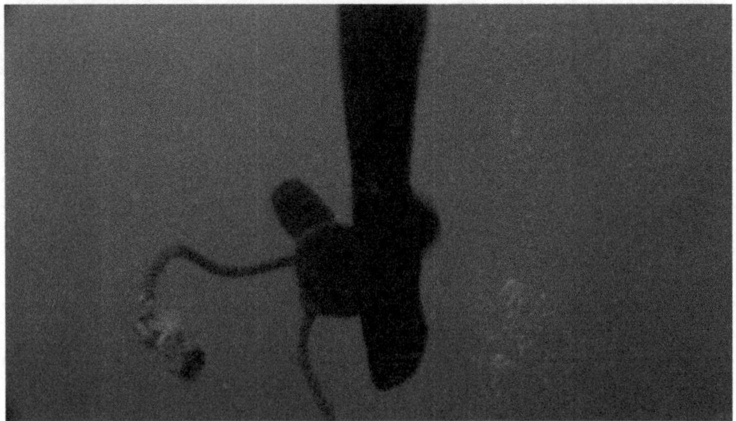

FIGURE 34 ***The Piano,*** ***1993.***

interested in sensations, feelings, and subtleties of her characters. As mentioned above, the eroticism of tactility is visible through many powerful close-ups, often emphasized by a preceding wide shot playing with the contrast of scale, a motive that runs through all of Campion's films and that lets us experience the character in a surprising distance-proximity sequence. (I will look at one of these examples from *Bright Star* more closely in Chapter 5, the book's conclusion.)

Overall, *The Piano* is a film that highlights and exposes to a wide audience in a visceral physical way to go back to Sobchack's reading of a sensual sense-making experience that to create a safe belonging and participation in a society, a woman needs a separated subjectivity. Ada achieves this separation from the "belly of the mother" by overcoming the violence of being chopped off a finger, which she turns into a way to escape her destiny, leaving the object of her attachment behind, the piano, and learning to speak for the first time. Just like the child who goes on their first voyage on her own, she has to confront herself with strangers she chooses to interact with, in this case the sexy George Baines, and who aren't chosen for her. During the making of this film, Jane Campion met and fell in love with the second unit director, Colin Englert, whom she married in 1992. At the end of the production, the couple expected a son, as already discussed earlier, but Jane lost the baby shortly after the film had come out—just like her mother Edith had lost her first son. While Campion won the Palme d'Or in Cannes for *The Piano*, the highest achievement of her career as a filmmaker, she also lost her baby the same year. Another bittersweet note was that, while she won the Palme d'Or, she had to share it ex aequo with *Farewell My Concubine* by Chen Kaige. The jury apparently could not give the Palme d'Or to *one* woman, but had to make it one woman and one other "other auteur." It would take another twenty years for Campion to be able to claim the stage of the international awards to herself. In 1994, she had another child, Alice, who was healthy and who is today a successful actress in her own right and was part of the cast of Campion's Short, *The Water Diary* (2006), the TV series *Top of the Lake* (2013–17), and her latest, *The Power of the Dog* (2021). Today, Alice is an independent film director in her own right.

The Portrait of a Lady, 1996

After *The Piano's* immense success, there was of course a great expectation for Campion's immediate next film, *The Portrait of a Lady*, based on Henry James's homonymous novel from 1881. Needless to say that it was impossible to meet the passionate fans' expectations. In fact, many people had an outright negative reaction to the film, which was unfortunate and certainly not fair to the film that was a direct continuation of Campion's auteurism.

Before I dive into the film's brief discussion, getting close to Campion's lead role Lady Isabel Archer, her inner life, and her sexual desires displayed on the screen, I want to discuss a brief history and discussions of representations of female sexuality in the literature of Henry James and his contemporaries that Campion drew from. It comes as no surprise that the historical tradition of literary accounts of female sexuality was in the firm hands of male writers. As Brian Stableford points out in his introduction to the latest English translation of Victor Margueritte's *Bacheloress* (*La Garçonne*, 1922), "France has an exceptionally rich tradition of extended character studies of women who kick over the traces of conventional sexual morality."[41] I want to recall some of these famous classics here: *The Story of the Chevalier des Grieux and Manon Lescaut* (1731) by the Abbé Antoine François Prévost, Émile Zola's *Thérèse Raquin* (1867), of course Gustave Flaubert's notorious *Madame Bovary* (1856), as well as the Goncourt brothers' *Renée Mauperin* (1864), and Joris-Karl Huysmans's *Marthe* (1876).

While England had a less prominent market for this kind of women's sexual character studies, Henry James's novel, *The Portrait of a Lady*, was published in 1881, inaugurating this booming sub-genre of women's (sexual) experiences to great acclaim. Only thirty years earlier, in 1851, the British philosopher and women's rights advocate Harriet Taylor Mill had written:

> Women, it is said, do not desire—do not seek, what is called their emancipation. [. . .] Custom hardens human beings to any kind of

> degradation, by deadening the part of their nature which would resist it. And the case of women is, in this respect, even a peculiar one, for no other inferior case that we have heard of have been taught to regard degradation as their honour.[42]

James's novel tells the story of a strong-willed young American woman from late nineteenth-century Albany, New York, Isabel Archer, who inherits a large fortune from her British uncle and is thrust into the high society of Europe (England and Italy), where she faces love and betrayal, searching for a new meaning in life. James's heroine refuses marriage proposals from the sickly Ralph Touchett, the refined Lord Warburton, and the boring Caspar Goodwood, but nevertheless ends up giving in to marriage to the seductive yet dangerous, Gilbert Osmond in Florence. Osmond reveals himself as a cruel husband who forces her into an unhappy life. Isabel becomes close to Osmond's daughter, Pansy, whom her father wants to get married to Lord Warburton, while he, however, only has eyes for Isabel. Campion's adaptation of the story isn't looking to blame the men for Isabel's fate of an unfulfilled life but rather turns the heroine into a driving force of her own destiny, and the film into a "girl's voyage towards darkness and underground regions. There is also a mythic dimension, with an awakening at the end."[43] Campion wanted to turn *The Portrait of a Lady* into an erotic story, particularly from a woman's perspective. She describes Isabel Archer as a "romantic addict," comparing her openly to herself, which explains why she holds her character responsible for her bad choices and life's disappointments. At the same time, Campion shows "a woman with very strong sexual aspirations, who wants to be loved and who feels frustrated [. . .] at her core, she is looking for passion."[44]

In Jane Campion's version of the novel, which she admits to have been a monumental task to turn into a filmic screenplay, she developed Isabel's sexual dimensions deeply and made the film about a passionate sexual woman, while Isabel's sexuality was only alluded to in the novel. Just like Ada, Isabel has lustful sexual fantasies. When Ada was shown in an auto-erotic sex scene, which she engages unwillingly with her husband Alisdair after he has just mutilated her by chopping up her finger as punishment for betraying him with George Baines, she was able to "talk back" in silence to her husband. Her fantasy realm saved her, and we experience Ada's self-satisfaction despite her husband's oppressive presence. Similarly, Isabel is imagining sexual satisfaction with three different men at once, when in real life she suffers one disappointment after the other one. In all of these sex scenes on-screen, Campion conflates the dream-sphere with reality, letting us in with the character's deepest unusual desires, which we experience entirely from her point of view and without judging her.

As Harriet Margolis and Jane Hughes[45] point out, *The Portrait of a Lady* is no longer a book by Henry James, but it becomes a film by Jane Campion, an auteur film, whose nature I have described in Chapter 2. Besides, it is now a film by "the director of *The Piano*." Margolis and Hughes further remark in the same breath, "Campion's auteurism makes her Portrait a work of art itself, rather than a poor relation of Henry James's original." I could not agree more with such assessment. As mentioned earlier, Campion is the first woman auteur who dared express herself in what I would label the "historical revisionist epic." To reiterate what I already said in this chapter's introduction: this was before Sofia Coppola's pop-history of *Marie Antoinette* (2006), before Céline Sciamma's acclaimed historical lesbian drama *Portrait of a Lady on Fire*, before Katharina Eyssen's Netflix series *The Empress* (2022) or Marie Kreutzer's *Corsage* (2022), both of which rewrote the life of Austrian empress Elisabeth with a modern feminist view.

The Portrait of a Lady is full of surprises. In fact, this historical film itself opens with the voice-over conversations of contemporary young Australian women who speak openly about their sexual desires and ideas of love. On the one hand, these frank testimonies seem to be coming out of their teenage fantasies, and on the other hand, they express a sophisticated knowledge of love. In an interview with Michael Ciment from 1996, Campion shares that the young women spoke off the cuff about their aspirations and sentimental experiences and weren't much directed by her.[46] The montage starts with a woman who states that "the best part of the kiss I think is when you see that head coming towards you and you know that you are going to get kissed." This statement of being the passive receiver of the kiss and not knowing how to properly consent to a proposed sexual gesture resonates strongly with a later fatal scene in the film when Osmond first declares his love and intended marriage to Isabel, which she refuses to hear. However, during the course of his courtship, which involves among other gestures, a seductive turning of the sun umbrella, Osmond, played brilliantly by the irresistible John Malkovich, leans forward to force a kiss onto Isabel. Isabel slowly gives in. This complex sentiment by a woman not wanting to disappoint the man who desires her, and hence becomes complicit while not expressing verbal or gestural consent, is further reflected in the continued opening montage's voice-over statements: "It means finding a mirror, the clearest and the most loyal mirror, and so when I love that person, I know they will shine that back to me." While Isabel thinks to have found this "mirror" of herself in the figure of Osmond, he actually turns out to be "a negative mirror-image of Isabel's spiritual aspirations."[47] Because of her idealization of this man, she made the wrong decision and chose exactly the *wrong* one, after refusing the kind but perhaps boring offers of Ralph Touchett, Lord Warburton, and Sir Goodwood. Coming back to the opening montage, the several women who are situated in the woods melt beautifully into the historical past through the eyes of our heroine, Isabel, now in full color and played in a stunning performance by the young Nicole Kidman (who was hesitant about the role initially). All women are looking intensely and mysteriously into the camera, at times dancing or listening to music on their walkmen. The times are reversed. The here and now of the lives of our contemporary Australian women is expressed with the crisp black-and-white archival-looking imagery that tells us that the "problem" women have with their own desire and with creating safe boundaries between themselves and their sexual partners hasn't changed at all. At the end of the montage, the camera zooms in onto a stunning close-up of Nicole Kidman's eyes, who are expressing confusion, desire, pain, and a quest . . . all at once. The colors have changed, and even though we are in a historical setting, her eyes are deep blue. The rawness of Kidman's eyes and face in general is refreshing to see, especially as Kidman's more recent career has made such a glimpse into her inner character difficult, due to the heavy use of Botox and cosmetic surgery (Figures 35–37).

This opening sequence did not meet many critics' positive reviews, as it was probably too experimental for a general and wide audience in the mid-nineties. I want to point out its resemblance to the opening sequence of *The Piano*, which I have analyzed above,

FIGURES 35, 36, AND 37 **The Portrait of a Lady, *1996.***

in that it shows a woman's direct perspective, in this case several women's, who are looking us straight in the eyes, revealing their inner struggles, excitements, joys, and pains of female embodiment. Both openings, *The Piano* and *The Portrait of a Lady*, are connected and direct quotations of Campion's end-sequence from her short, *A Girl's*

Own Story, during which we see sisters Pam and Prue and other girls sing together. I want to point out that this end-sequence also includes the bewildered face of Pam while a male hand wanders over her caressingly. In my opinion, all of these opening or ending sequences express the same question of a woman's body and embodiment: who has the right to touch or look at it? The desire for the visual close-encounter with the character's eyes, however, is something that was already present in *Peel*, discussed in Chapter 2's Figure 5–8 sequence, where it served the purpose of the estrangement from the character rather than the feminist critique of looking and not being seen (Figures 38 and 39).

For *The Portrait of a Lady*, Campion went back to writer Laura Jones, who had written the screenplay for *An Angel at My Table*. While I won't have time in this chapter's context to compare the original book with Jones's screenplay in detail, I want to point out that Jones enhanced the already open ending that Henry James had given the novel. The unanswered and open questions at the end of Campion's film are as follows: "will Isabel remain in England? Will she become receptive to Goodwood's overtures? Will she return to

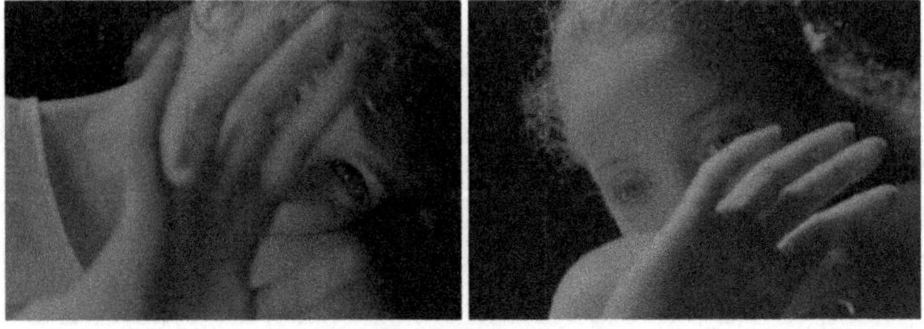

FIGURES 38 AND 39 **A Girl's Own Story,** ***1984.***

Italy and either confront Osmond, or reconcile to her life with him, or rescue Pansy?"[48]

While the novel presents the disturbing kiss by Caspar Goodwood "like white lightning"—in the film, Osmond's kiss, which I already alluded to above, remains enigmatic and does not provide any answers to Isabel's future. Yet, the scene with the first kiss by Gilbert Osmond is a key moment, where a woman first says "no" to a man's proposal but then acts "yes." The man is Osmond who declares his love for her. Even though she says "no" to his declaration and wants to hear no more, her character clearly melts inside, as her "desire to be loved," a key theme for Campion in this film,[49] is what drives every pore of Isabel's being and also the story. While the film has a period background, it becomes very clear in this moment that it is about the intimacy between the characters and not about the time it is playing in. This reveals, in my opinion, the film's feminist nature in that this heroine, unlike Ada, does not come to a clear "solution" of her time. Even more controversially, Jane Campion's Isabel is fascinated by images of domination and submission. At her core, Isabel is looking for passion, sexual fulfillment, but of course, this is not something she can just live, as it is after all, the 1870s, during the Victorian era. The film responds to this repression by revealing us Isabel's fantasies on the screen already through the very opening sequence, in the black-and-white home movie-style images, a "mental diary," as Campion called them. In one of them, Isabel is able to say what she did not say in the scene: "I am absolutely in love with you." A sentence she never dared to say when she was "being kissed."

The secrecy in the film and the things that aren't being said lead to an open-endedness and perhaps undecidedness of the film's ending.

As a result, many critics described the film as cold and unerotic. Alistair Fox, in his psychoanalytical reading of Isabel's character, reads her wondrous and perhaps undecided nature as a "yearning to enter into a relationship with an older man who is capable of repairing the lack she experienced as a child."[50] In other words, for Fox, Isabel is trying to "fix" the older man, by which she hopes to heal her own wounds; this is a motive that I already discussed with Ruth's love affair with her healer and the father figure in *Holy Smoke!* in Chapter 2.

Visually and cinematographically speaking, the film enhances the undecidedness and unresolvedness of the character by showing the characters in claustrophobic spaces that express confinement and darkness. Cinematographer Stuart Dryburgh, who also shot *The Piano* with Campion, points out that while he shot the film in a widescreen format, the composition does not play as much with contrasting scales and proportions, as in other Campion films, but features tight shots that leave little space around faces. Imperceptible slow motions, which have been compared to Peter Weir's *Picnic at Hanging Rock* discussed in Chapter 1, express the sense of mystery and create a mood of uncertainty. Dryburgh also enhanced the darkness around the characters by backlighting the scenes, at times creating dark silhouettes of their figures, and he reports to have been inspired by Dutch masters such as Rembrandt and Vermeer for the use of chiaroscuro.[51] By creating these "gothic spaces," Isabel's powerlessness comes to full cinematic fruition. Unlike with the ending of *The Piano*, where Ada and Baines were able to save themselves through their positive love, *The Portrait of a Lady* points to the complexity around female empowerment: "It is a film that refuses resolutely to represent an easy image of female empowerment by the conventions of a kind of woman's film."[52]

This complexity is important to Campion, and she has little interest in the traditional costume drama, dismissing the rush of Jane Austen adaptations as "very soft." By contrast, for her, James is very modern because he's already tearing apart the fairytale. He's saying: "Be real. Life is hard. . . . No one's going to get the right person."[53] What Campion loves about James is that he plots a life in terms of the spiritual journey. "Isabel Archer starts out on a false journey—in the pursuit of worldly knowledge, and she can't even imagine what it is she wants to be knowing and learning. What she does find out is who she is."[54] Campion identified closely with Isabel's journey. She loved Europe. But when she tried to live in England, she got very depressed. When she tried to live in Italy, she suffered from the cold Italian winters without heaters. She also needed to feed her relationship with the sky. "One can have a very psychic relationship with the sky,"[55] she says, and with this, she feels very much an island girl.

The metaphorical symmetry of the trees is one of the important visual cues in *The Portrait of a Lady*. Lord Warburton proposes to Isabel at the beginning in the blushing summer of the outdoors. The same tree, during winter, is where Isabel sits down in sadness after the funeral of her cousin Ralph Touchett, who had asked her to become his wife. The change of season expresses the harsh reality that Isabel cannot go back to a better life decision, as she refused both men and married the *wrong* one, as stated above (Figures 40 and 41).

One film critic claimed that *The Portrait of a Lady* would appeal more to the head than to the heart, making for a "portrait that seems somewhat less than complete."[56] As said earlier, it would have been impossible to satisfy an audience or any critic with a film that would come close to being as beloved as *The Piano*. Sadly, and definitely

FIGURES 40 AND 41 The Portrait of a Lady, *1996.*

not fair to the quality of the film, *The Portrait of a Lady* opened predominantly to negative critiques, and just like her next film, *Holy Smoke!*, had a difficult time making a profit in the box office, despite its remarkable cast: Nicole Kidman (playing Isabel Archer), John Malkovich (playing Gilbert Osmond), Viggo Mortensen, and Sir John Gielgud.

The Embodied Gaze

This chapter looked at Campion's films, highlighting the condition of women's bodies, their state of sexuality, and implicitly critiquing their lack of freedom in the traditionally male workspaces. This is a kind of feminism that is concerned with the question of speaking *from within femininity*—and hereby creating a unique genre that often blends tragic melodrama with romantic wish-fulfillment fantasy. Campion's embodied gaze onto women's bodies and life stories further lets women escape and liberate themselves from what Fox had previously "diagnosed" as the disturbed family romance, including her characters engaging in incest fantasies or searching for father substitutes. The heroines in these mid-career films are both free and fatherless, and in many of them, the family backgrounds have been entirely removed. The condition of all of these women's freedom is that they become self-aware and embodied subjects. What is more, these embodied characters have not only freed themselves in a narrative way by being able to pursue their professions and love lives, but they have been able to emotionally repair themselves, as Fox has pointed out the case of Ada and Isabel.[57]

In *2 Friends*, the negative and traumatizing bodily experiences of testing the slippery grounds of sexuality have caused a sense of isolation and failure for the character, and while Kelly "failed" in the real world, Janet, Ada, and Isabel were able to "make it." What Kelly and Ada have in common is an experience of abuse, which in both cases, while in completely different ways, has been obfuscated and remains narratively untold and only implied or alluded to in these films. This might be the case to mirror the assault victim's perception and her repressed trauma, as many victims don't recall what happened to them. The success of *The Piano* lies in the fact that despite the character's untold traumatic experience at a young age, the film shows a later part of her life during which she overcomes her physical trauma (including her muteness, which is represented as a direct effect from the traumatizing event). The film's happy ending wasn't Campion's original intention in the first draft of the screenplay, but it is in my view the explanation for its huge commercial success. For that reason, I would qualify *The Piano* to be the first and only one of Campion's films that qualifies as what we today call an empowerment film.

Mothers not standing by their daughters is another Campion motive that is broken in *The Piano*. Ada, even though her daughter Flora betrays her by revealing her relationship with George Baines to her stepfather Alisdair Stewart, does not hold this betrayal against her young daughter. In this way, Ada overcomes several of Campion's "character hurdles," which I attribute to her portrayal of a happy sexuality that she grows into throughout the film. Like in the films from Chapter 1 and Chapter 2, there are continued visual themes in the films discussed in Chapter 3: women's legs, an attention to such primordial elements as water, and in *The Piano*, this includes the iconic image of a woman's leg and shoe first drowning underwater but then liberating itself to swim back to the surface in order to survive and *live*. In fact, if there is one motive that unites these films discussed above, it is women's desire to *live*. After these important films of Campion's mid-career, she become one of the most important directors in the world.

4

The Redefining Gaze

Late-Career Features and Television Productions 2003–21

If the previous two chapters argued that Campion's cinema can be regarded as having articulated both a transgressive and an embodied feminine gaze, in the present chapter I will show how some of her later works, from her 2003 adaptation of Susanna Moore's novel *In the Cut*, through her limited series *Top of the Lake*, and finally to her Best-Picture-winning *The Power of the Dog*, step into existing genres and redefine them from the inside out, using the very problem of cinematic and televisual genre as a way of interrogating implicitly male approaches embedded in those genres, and redefining them to make way for a different kind of storytelling.

In the Cut, 2003

Campion's noir thriller, and as McHugh points out,[1] her first clear-cut genre film, *In the Cut* largely flopped at the box office, just like *The Portrait of a Lady*, but in this case, it was because of the controversy around the explicitly narrated sexuality of the female lead character, Frannie, played by Meg Ryan. Ryan, eager to work with Campion so as to step out of her typecasting as America's sweetheart in films like *Sleepless in Seattle*, *You've Got Mail*, and *When Harry Met Sally*, arguably destroyed her career in the process. While Ryan didn't show her bare breasts in this film, her character Frannie lives out her unusual sexual desires in a way that, to put it in the terms of Alistair Fox's psychoanalytic reading, brings the "family romance" to a complete collapse.

In the film, which I have discussed in my book *The Cosmetic Gaze: Body Modification and the Construction of Beauty* (2012), Frannie Avery, portrayed by Ryan, is a Brooklyn teacher who finds herself drawn to a police chief, portrayed by Mark Ruffalo, who is diligently working to unravel a string of heinous crimes targeting women, including the grisly dismemberment of victims' bodies. The film's thematic fixations, alongside its depictions of both actual and symbolic mutilations, highlight Campion's contemplation of the brutality inherent in the portrayal of women's fragmented bodies that is so central to the thriller genre. And yet Campion's redefining gaze isn't merely critical of such violence; her film doesn't merely reverse or satirize the dynamics we come to expect from it. Rather, *In the Cut*, building on a theme Campion clearly found in Susanna Moore's 1995 novel of the same name, explores the erotics of the genre itself by asking what it is about showing the desire to cut women's bodies that so effectively attracts the audience's interest.

To do this, *In the Cut* must explore the complexities surrounding the representation of femininity, especially female sexuality, which is the focus of Moore's novel. Moore's novel, which I want to highlight, already established a significant correlation between the fragmented depiction of the female body—embodied by the murdered Angela Sands—and erotic desire, as experienced by the protagonist Frannie toward detective James A. Malloy, who is investigating the case for Manhattan's Washington Square district. Here is the dialogue between Frannie and Malloy as written by Moore:

> "How was she killed?"
> "Her throat was cut." He paused. "And then she was disarticulated."
> What a good word, I thought. Disarticulated.
> He slid the notebook back into his pocket and took two cuff links from another pocket and turned down the sleeves of his shirt, and I remembered that it was masculine gestures that aroused me.[2]

The word "disarticulation" captivates Frannie, an English teacher with an interest in slang, who keeps a lexicon where she documents ambivalent and suggestive terms like "*skins*, n.; sex from a female (as in 'getting some skins from the pretties'); or, *to do*, v., to fuck; *to do*, v., to kill."[3] She experiences a mixture of threat and repulsion from "disarticulation," yet it paradoxically stirs her arousal.

Indeed, the ambivalent desire woven throughout the novel propels its narrative. It not only delves into the gruesome acts of a serial killer who meticulously dismembers his victims but also exposes the verbal dissection of femininity by the characters. For instance, during one conversation between detectives Malloy and Rodriguez,

> Rodriguez looked away from the girl and said, "You know, all you really need is two tits, a hole and a heartbeat."

> Malloy said mildly, "You don't really need the tits."
>
> Rodriguez said, "You don't even need the heartbeat."[4]

Similarly adopting an aggressively misogynist tone, Pauline, a nightclub dancer and Frannie's friend (in the film she becomes her stepsister, the "double" character in the character of Pauline Avery), says in a conversation with Frannie: "There are some people . . . usually women, whom you can fuck only if you have permission to kill them immediately afterward."[5]

The femicidal violence of these sentences, even ones spoken by women in the novel, begs the question of why Campion would be attracted to turning the novel into a film in the first place. According to Fox, the material was perfect for Campion:

> First, it contained many elements of sexual fantasy, including the subject's release from repression through a fantasized reversal of customary inhibitions, and the eventual punishment that answers to the guilt of the fantasist for entertaining the possibilities of such a breakout. [. . .] Second, for Campion pornography and eroticism are ways of challenging the repressive mores entrenched in the two Antipodean societies she has experienced, and it is not surprising that she identified In the Cut as a potential vehicle for her resistance against conventional taboos, which she considers prudish and dishonest.[6]

I would like to add that the answer for Campion's choice also lies in how Moore's novel finds in the language of the streets and the language of law enforcement precisely the linkage between violence toward women's bodies and sexual desire that Campion uses her film to explore. In other words, is there not already at the very level at which society talks about women, and hence in the language with which both men and women come into consciousness, an implicit fusion of sexual desire with violence toward women's bodies? And, if that is the case, and if women too are socialized within this discourse, how is it possible to define a feminine sexuality that would be free of masculine menace?

In these instances and many others in the novel, femininity is dissected through verbal blades, mirroring the literal dismemberment of female bodies by the serial killer. In the novel, cutting doesn't occur in a literal sense only. The misogynist language of Detective Malloy "cuts" into Frannie's thoughts. At the same time, these linguistic cuts stimulate her, arouse her, as is shown by Frannie's linguistic dictionary. Her desire is rooted in the idea of being the subject of dissection, a theme reiterated when she finds herself under the killer's knife.

> I did not feel the razor when he cut me, only knew it an instant later with the sudden rush of heat and pain, the sting of it, the warm blood slaking down my arms and over my hands. It didn't hurt that much after I got used to it. It wasn't a bad cut. Not too bad. He didn't mean to cut me, he said. But he couldn't help it.[7]

Likewise, when Frannie has sex with Detective Malloy, the language continues to be fragmented. It is not their whole bodies that are at play here, but only particular body parts: "He let his arm fall from my neck, down across my chest, until his hand was on my breast, his fingers finding the nipple. He pulled me back against him. He had an erection. I could feel it."[8] Accordingly, Frannie's initial intimate encounter with Malloy centers on his knowledge of female anatomy—a skill he acquired at a young age from an older woman—rather than her physical appearance, overall looks, or even her personality.

Therefore, the fragmented, "disarticulated" female form emerges as the foundation from which femininity is articulated. Indeed, we come to understand that femininity itself exists "in the cut." Near the novel's conclusion, as Frannie faces the serial killer's blade, she utters these words:

> Cutting me. He doesn't like it. I don't like it, either. I have a new word for the dictionary. Malloy told it to me. A street word. A word used by gamblers for when you be peepin', he said. In the cut. From the vagina. A place to hide. To hedge your bet. But someplace safe, someplace free from harm.[9]

It is "in the cut"—this perilously secure space—where Frannie discovers her sexual desire. This is the vantage point from which she spied on a woman who would later be the novel's first casualty. This incident serves as the pivotal moment that propels the narrative forward. It is no mere coincidence that both the woman and Frannie face a similar fate at the hands of a serial killer, being cut to death. But there's more they share, a detail Frannie reveals to the readers: "a secret that was exciting because it was dangerous to both of us: A woman with red hair had been on her knees with his red cock in her red mouth a few hours before having her throat cut and her arms and legs pulled from their sockets."[10] In the film's version of this peeping Tom scene, Frannie walks through the dark basement of a café, where she is meeting with her student, following the sounds of the sex scene. Once she discovers where the sound comes from, she first backs away but then gets visually aroused, as seen in Figure 42.

How does Campion's filmmaking take up the provocative question of Moore's novel, the suturing of feminine desire with masculine violence? How does it redefine an equation essential to the very genre of the thriller? It does so by, in essence, using Moore's own metaphor and title, and viewing that desire and those relations from *within the cut*. In this way, Campion again creates a specifically female gaze, even as she explores a very problematic cinematic genre, one built upon the premises of a violent, male gaze.

In the film, a key factor that brings a feminine perspective to life is the cinematography by Dion Beebe. Frequently utilizing a handheld camera, the film often employs simpler lenses that are well-suited to this style, allowing the operator to manually fine-tune the focus.[11] However, the ingenuity in Campion's selection of a camera that articulates the notion of fragmented femininity has been overlooked or misunderstood by mainstream media. As the critic Andy Klein wrote, "It's not just the opening shots here that are blurry

FIGURE 42 In the Cut, *2003*.

and unsteady: The point and perspective of the whole film remain unfocused throughout."[12]

To delve deeper into the camera work, consider the film's portrayal of the book's first scene of sexual arousal. In this scene, during their initial meeting in Frannie's Lower Manhattan apartment, Malloy questions her as a possible witness to Angela Sands's murder: "You don't remember seeing anything, hearing anything?" Frannie looks at his tattoo and says: "Can you tell me how it happened?" Malloy: "The throat was cut and then she was disarticulated." As soon as the word "cut" is spoken, the camera shifts to Frannie. Then, when the term "disarticulated" is used, it pans back to the detective, who, in Campion's adaptation, has been given a different name: Giovanni instead of James.[13] Frannie jots down the word "disarticulated," and the camera zooms in on the word written by hand, concluding the initial erotic sequence. Significantly later in the story, after being mugged on the street and just before her first intimate moment with Malloy, Frannie poses another question to the detective: "How was that girl killed?"

The intimacy between Malloy and Frannie, which unfolds soon after this inquiry, intertwines with discussions about the violent deeds of a serial killer and the fragmented female form. Amplifying this suspense inherent in the notion of the "lady killer," whose meaning fluctuates between "killing a woman" and "arousing a woman," the film adaptation introduces an even more enigmatic detective who, for the audience, could potentially be the killer.[14] Only near the conclusion of the film does the viewer become fully immersed in the narrative world, where Malloy is simply portrayed as a detective.

The lingering resonance of the word "disarticulation," stemming from their initial meeting, serves as the catalyst for the first intimate encounter between Frannie and Malloy: "What exactly does disarticulation mean?" Frannie asks. Malloy explains: "He is trying to dismember the female body." Almost at once he continues: "Show me. How did he [the mugger] hold you?" Malloy proceeds to reenact the assault with Frannie. Adopting the mugger's approach, he approaches her from behind, touching her breast. At this juncture, the camera shifts from its neutral perspective and zooms in on the erotic encounter, capturing intricate details of their bodies, including Malloy's (ambiguous) tattoo. Frannie retrieves a condom from the adjacent room and undresses. Malloy then issues commands: "Take those [panties] off." Subsequently, he caresses her buttocks and begins to orally stimulate her genitals, eliciting sexual pleasure. This explicit depiction underscores the direct link between female sexuality and the fragmented female identity, epitomizing the concept of being "cut up" in its most literal sense.

Amidst a crime scene featuring yet another dismembered female body, marked by the unsettling sight of body parts being extracted from a public washing machine by a crime scene investigator, Malloy receives a call from Frannie. Once more, the themes of dismemberment and eroticism converge within a single scene. Malloy proceeds to explain, "Another girl has been murdered." Frannie: "What happened?" Malloy: "She has been cut up. We can't find her head. The fucking press is all over." Malloy then shifts gears: "Can you do something for me, will you?" Now, he directs her on how to pleasure herself. The crimson hues from the crime scene flash intermittently as Frannie obediently follows Malloy's commands:

"Slip your middle finger in that pussy that I like." Visually, Malloy's arousal gets connected to the crime scene, as we can see in the below frame. What is more, the "messages" that we read, in this case as mirror images, are telling us "something," adding to the film's linguistic enigma and also reflecting the main character's linguistic profession (Figure 43).

The subsequent crime scene intrudes more deeply into Frannie's personal narrative. Just prior to her discovery of her stepsister Pauline's dismembered remains, the camera tenderly explores her sexualized form. Following the grim discovery, Frannie is escorted to the police station, where Malloy endeavors to soothe her frayed nerves. In her state of confusion and trauma, Frannie, now harboring suspicions of Malloy being the killer, seeks detailed clarification on her sister's demise—wanting to ascertain if it was swift. Malloy, despite her growing suspicions, proceeds to explain the circumstances in painstaking detail:

FIGURE 43 *In* The Cut, *2003.*

> This guy, this guy must have known her. He strangled her until she lost consciousness probably in the bedroom, then he dragged her to the bathroom, cut her throat, cut through the windpipe, the jugular, the epiglottis, the hyoid, the tongue, he held her by the hair and cut all around. This guy likes blood. When he got to the vertebrae, he needed a bigger knife to cut through that and he had one. He pulled the drain in the sink before he left, so he left us nothing that could help us. It scares me that this guy knows about drains.[15]

Unlike during their sex-talk, Malloy's aggressive language bothers Frannie. When she asks suspiciously where he was when Pauline was murdered, he tells her "working." "You mean getting blow jobs?" she asks him. Malloy then initiates a conversation with her about whether there even exists such a thing as a "bad blow job." Frannie is struck by Malloy's choice of words, particularly by his statement about having "no sense of cock." However, this time, instead of sexually arousing Frannie, Malloy's confidence regarding the crime further fuels her suspicion that he might be the murderer. She concludes their exchange by bluntly asking, "Did you kill her?" Malloy sidesteps the question, opting to hand her over to his female colleague to escort her home. He expresses his frustration and humiliation with a terse command: "get the fuck out of here!"

The pivotal scene that perhaps best elucidates the dynamic between Frannie and Malloy occurs in one of the last chapters of Moore's novel, titled "Frannie Is in Control." Here, Frannie restrains the detective by handcuffing him to a pipe in her apartment and proceeds to pleasure herself using Malloy's body as a sexual object. In the film adaptation, this scene faithfully mirrors the novel. It is during this intimate encounter that Malloy employs the phrase "in the cut," referencing their mutual inclination toward observation, as previously detailed: "You like watching," I [Frannie] said. "Yeah," he said, "I like it in the cut."[16] Malloy is "in the cut" of Frannie's femininity, where she finds pleasure. Frannie is "in the cut" of her own vulnerability and openness. The camera delicately captures the unfolding moment, occasionally blurring, suggesting a closeness almost uncomfortably near. Both characters are depicted fragmentarily, showcasing Frannie's shoulder, mouth, and nose, alongside Malloy's obscured hair from behind.

As in other filmic tales and literary adaptations by Campion, such as *An Angel at My Table*, *The Piano*, and *The Portrait of a Lady*, *In the Cut* scrutinizes a romantic narrative that revolves around a woman's perception of the world and her unique perspective. Frannie's personal narrative is hinted at early in the film through a dream sequence, depicted cinematically in black and white. It recounts the tale of her father, portrayed as a graceful ice skater, who romantically proposes to her mother by kneeling on the ice and presenting a dazzling engagement ring. However, the complication arises as he impulsively proposes to her after just seeing her on the ice, while he had been engaged to another woman with whom he was dancing. For the romantic gesture to occur, he must forsake his previous relationship and inflict pain upon a woman who loves him. Essentially, the romantic ideal is only achievable through significant suffering. This metaphor closely mirrors the narrative of *In the Cut* itself, where romanticism and sexuality intertwine with themes of murder and tragedy.

The father's proposal, as well as his breaking of the previous engagement, occurs on the ice—a surface that is blank like a "tabula rasa," hard, and initially frictionless until the skates etch and mold their weight into it. In the film's sound design, this engraving is depicted loudly and forcefully; we hear the skates slicing into the ice. It is within these cuts on the ice that the myth unfolds itself. As Campion elucidates in the director's commentary, Frannie finds herself ensnared in the paradox of romanticizing her parents' love story, which stemmed from and is inherently linked to the disappointment of another individual. As the film progresses, we learn that Pauline's fate aligns precisely with this tradition. Frannie's father left her mother and had another child, Pauline, with another woman, whom he never married. As Frannie reveals in a conversation with her stepsister, this disappointment ultimately led to their mother's demise.

Certainly, Frannie hints at numerous potential reasons for her psychological fragility and, ultimately, for the plight of womanhood throughout the entirety of the film. For instance, following Pauline's demise and her subsequent presence at the police station, Frannie divulges a crucial anecdote from her past to Malloy. "When I was thirteen my father left me in Geneva. He was called away to Washington for five days. He said later that it never occurred to him that I wouldn't be all right. Pauline said later that I failed to take advantage of the situation, that I should have ordered 100 boxes of chocolate and made a snowman."[17] Another instance in the film where Campion subverts romantic mythology appears in a conversation between Frannie and her eccentric ex-boyfriend, John Graham, who poses a question to her: "Did I ever tell you that my mother used to dress me in girls' blouses?" John explains his struggles and eccentricities by attributing them to his mother, rather than his father, claiming that she played a significant role in shaping him into someone different.

The film's concluding sequence can be interpreted as an allegory for Frannie's female plight. We witness Frannie, who has triumphed over the unexpected serial killer, Malloy's own police partner Detective Rodriguez, making her way back from the lighthouse. As she nears Lower Manhattan, the camera shifts to view her from the vantage point of her own apartment. Frannie traverses her backyard, adorned with white blossoms, before entering the apartment and reclining beside the handcuffed Malloy. The door closes. This sequence echoes imagery from the film's outset, particularly scenes of Lower Manhattan. In those initial moments, these images were juxtaposed with Pauline's stroll through the same blooming garden on her way to visit her stepsister, Frannie. For Campion, this opening sequence holds special significance:

> It really is in a nutshell the whole film because it talks about the girl looking lost. The blossoms come down and it's a beautiful transcendent moment in their own little Manhattan garden. Frannie looks out the window and mistakes the blossoms for snow. It's all a series of mistaken identity. We think we have seen something and then we find out we haven't. Most human knowing is faulty and most of the time wrong. Everyone is in a private dream, a private mythology. The dream Frannie is trying to free herself from, she inherits from her mother. It's the romantic mythology from her mother's childhood. The romance is attractive to Frannie, but on the other hand she saw the mother die because she was so betrayed by the father.[18]

Campion's cinematic narrative immerses us in the mythic realm of romance, not unsimilar to *The Piano*. But in *In the Cut*, the yearning for a "happy ending" is assumed and subtly ever-present entirely on the mythical level, and never in the narrative of the film: the father marries his ideal woman, Frannie's mother, bears a child with her, and remains by her side until death parts them. However, in this film and its redefining gaze, "the cut" imposes itself upon this myth. Paradoxically, the romance between Frannie and Malloy is ignited solely because of the cut and unfolds within the disruption and injury of the very myth itself. Simply put, the myth can only take root on the precarious foundation of the cut, and therefore is perpetually threatened by its own dissolution. The destiny of feminine subjectivity is to fervently desire both aspects, despite their inherent contradiction: the mythical completeness of romance and its inevitable disintegration within the cut. While the conscious mind is drawn to the former, the latter represents the realm of the unconscious and sexual desire.

What Campion conveys with "we think we have seen something and then we find out we haven't," beautifully translates to the myth of fractured familial happiness, and in this case the debunking of the reliable police myth, since Detective Rodriguez, the killer, was ever so close to the main Detective character Malloy. Her characters are thrust into their environments, possessing fragments of their past, as revealed in Frannie's dreams. Yet, they navigate a path marked by chance occurrences. Frannie seeks clues within the realm of language poetry, which she avidly collects, hoping to uncover meaning and certainty. Instead, she encounters nothing but contingency. Descending the steps at the bar, she unwittingly becomes a witness to a sexual encounter between a female victim and her assailant.

Believing she recognizes the tattoo on Malloy's arm, she later realizes it belongs to Detective Rodriguez. In essence, the act of cutting can also be interpreted as castration. After all, it was the castrated mother who gave birth to Frannie, exposing her to the radical contingency of her own existence. It is no coincidence that *In the Cut* ends with an eerie rearrangement of Ray Evans's own *Que será será* (1956).[19]

> When I grew up and fell in love and asked my sweetheart what lies ahead. Will there be rainbows day after the day? Here is what my sweetheart said: Que será será, whatever will be will be. The future's not ours to see. Que será será. Now I have children of my own. They ask their mother what will I be. Will I be pretty will I be rich? I tell them tenderly. Que será será, whatever will be will be. The future's not ours to see. Que será será.[20]

While Fox pairs *In the Cut* with *Holy Smoke!* and both films' associated trauma with the father figures and their abusive behaviors toward the mothers, I want to argue that in this film, the female subject is not merely confined to a desiring femininity. Rather, heteronormative femininity is explored as a position entangled within the very gaze itself. There exists no external vantage point to this position, only an "in the cut." We are confronted with a femininity that inherently comprises fragmentation from the outset. There exists no complete female body on screen; it has never existed. In this emblematic film, femininity is articulated and depicted in bloody fragments to underscore the impossibility of an external gaze upon femininity. This is shown with a cinematography emphasizing the blurring of the obfuscated gaze onto the female body (Figure 44).

Being "in the cut" can be described as the place of female interiority from which *In the Cut* reports. It is in this sense that *In the Cut* is a

FIGURE 44 In the Cut, *2003.*

narrative continuation of the foregrounding of the female voice that she has shown in all her films from *Sweetie* to *An Angel at My Table* to *The Piano* and *The Portrait of a Lady*. All of these films have made use of their main protagonists' voice-over narration, which brings us into the psychic space of the character. What is more, in *In the Cut* this space is also shown as a place of ambiguity itself, a place that we cannot truly see until we cut it open.

Top of the Lake, 2013–17

In November 1977, a thirteen-year-old girl named Megumi Yokota, from Niigata, Japan, vanished without a trace. It was later confirmed that she was taken by North Korean spies to help North Korea learn Japanese language and habits. A year after the release of *In the Cut*, Jane Campion was credited as the executive producer on the documentary film *Abduction: The Megumi Yokota Story* (2006). Perhaps something in the story of the disappearance of a young girl stuck with Campion for years afterward. For in 2013, she released a limited television series, the first since *An Angel at My Table* more than twenty years earlier, that, for its part, redefined the TV detective series.

Set in a remote town in New Zealand, *Top of the Lake* tells the story of Detective Robin Griffin, played by Elisabeth Moss, who returns to her hometown to visit her ailing mother. Her visit coincides with the mysterious disappearance of a pregnant twelve-year-old girl named Tui. As Robin becomes deeply involved in the case, she encounters a web of interconnected characters, including Tui's troubled family, a group of eccentric women living in a women's commune called Paradise, and a menacing local crime lord named Matt Mitcham, played by a brilliant and menacing Peter Mullan. Alongside her investigation, Robin grapples with personal demons from her own past, including trauma related to her own experiences with sexual assault.

As it turns out, Robin's recovered memories of her assault at the hands of a group of boys from the town she has returned to will play a key role in Campion's redefining of the TV detective genre. Indeed, key to Robin's drive to crack the case of the sexual assault of Tui is precisely her own status as a victim of a sexual assault. True to her style, then, Campion's approach to the detective genre is to redefine it from the perspective of the victim of violence.

As the search for Tui intensifies, Robin discovers a series of shocking and parallel revelations that challenge her perceptions of justice, morality, and the nature of evil. Specifically, she discovers that the kind police chief who has supported her work not only drugged her in order to assault her, but he himself runs a child prostitution ring (reminiscent of the double-edged Detective Rodriguez figure). And just as the head of local law enforcement is revealed to be the source of crime, it is the patriarchal head of Tui's family, Matt Mitchell, who impregnated her. Searching for the baby Tui bore alone in the woods to kill it and remove the evidence of his crime, Matt is confronted by his daughter Tui, who shoots and kills him.

Ultimately, Robin's personal history as a survivor of sexual violence when she was fifteen imbues her character with a unique vulnerability that paradoxically becomes a source of strength. Her firsthand experience with trauma allows her to empathize with victims in ways that her male colleagues cannot, enabling her to perceive nuances and hidden truths that others overlook, and giving her a distinct advantage in cracking the case of Tui's rape. Her intimate understanding of the psychological impact of sexual violence allows her to navigate the complexities of the investigation with a level of insight and sensitivity that proves instrumental in unraveling the truth.

Furthermore, Robin's status as a survivor of sexual assault instills in her the drive to confront the dark underbelly of her community with a fearless determination. Unlike her peers, Robin is not intimidated by the taboo subject matter surrounding sexual abuse and exploitation. Instead, her own experiences fuel her to resolve and seek justice for Tui and other victims who have suffered similar fates. In this way, her vulnerability becomes a catalyst for uncovering the hidden depths of depravity that surround her, even in the most unlikely places. Most pointedly, being forced to confront her past trauma head-on leads her to dismantle the facade of authority and respectability maintained by police chief Al Parker, exposing him as the true orchestrator of a heinous child prostitution ring. In the end, it is Robin's experience as a victim that underlies her specific power.

Elisabeth Moss's star-making turn as Detective Robin Griffin, along with its eerie twist on the TV detective thriller that Campion, along with her co-writer and former partner Gerard Lee, who she had written *Sweetie* with, imbued it with, made *Top of the Lake* a smash success, garnering eight Emmy awards and reigniting the popularity of limited series in the age of prestige television.[21] Four years later, Moss returned to the small screen as Robin Griffin in a second season of *Top of the Lake*. As in the first season, women are both victims and victors, as Robin, now back in Sydney, Australia, teams up with an awkward, pregnant police officer named Miranda to investigate the body of a Chinese woman (hence, the title of the second series "China Girl") that has washed ashore in a suitcase.

Unfortunately, the attempt to replicate the patterns and themes of *Top of the Lake* in a new environment failed to replicate the success of the first series. As a review in *The Atlantic* argued, "in *China Girl*, set in the much larger city of Sydney, the show's continued presentation of men as rapists, pimps, cheats, and murderers is so committed it starts to become comical."[22] Indeed, it is likely that the revelation of Robin's status as a victim of sexual violence in the first season, so crucial for the original show's impact, left the second season with less to work with and ultimately undermined the power of the narrative and diminished the impact of its social critique. While the series continued to explore themes of sexual abuse, exploitation, and gender power dynamics, Robin's established history as a survivor sapped the emotional resonance that characterized her journey in the first season. As a result, the continued presence of male perpetrators in the storyline lacked the same sharpness as the revelations of the first season. The theme of the power of victimhood that Campion had been cultivating and exploring for years would need one more film, the one that would win her highest accolades, to reach its fruition.

The Power of the Dog, 2021

Campion's redefining of victimhood as a potential source of power in *Top of the Lake* is the reason that series serves as a pivot to move from *In the Cut*—where her adaptation of a novel's exploration of feminine desire at the nexus of male violence and victimhood used cinema's language to locate her own perspective within that of the victim of violence—to *The Power of the Dog*, the culminating film of this study, in which that very same perspective is used to turn the most stereotypical of male genres, the Western, inside out. Jane Campion's *The Power of the Dog*, for which she returns to author the screenplay on her own, can be seen in the lineage of queer Westerns from Ang Lee's *Broke Back Mountains* to Pedro Almodóvar's recent short, *Strange Way of Life* (2023). While Almodóvar's Western short carries the recognizable postmodern irony of its famed auteur—the short was shot with a technicolor visual palette, and scored to the classic Santaolalla's guitar pick. For her part, Campion reinvented her auteurism with *The Power of the Dog*. Indeed, in Campion's Oscar-winning film, based on the homonymous novel by Thomas Savage from 1967,[23] she not only again adapted a novel into her own cinematic auteur language, but—similarly to how she did with James's *The Portrait of a Lady*—translated it into a story of contemporary questions about sexual freedom, gender relations, and sexual orientation. She also reinvented the narrative structure of all of her films as for the first time the main protagonist is not only a man but also the violent figure himself and the source of the other characters' terror. He only becomes the one who is violated at the very end of the film in a surprising twist.

The Power of the Dog, which has been described as a "gothic western,"[24] follows the complex dynamics within a wealthy Montana ranching family in the 1920s. Brothers Phil and George Burbank, played by Benedict Cumberbatch and Jesse Plemons respectively, run the ranch together. When George marries Rose, played by Kirsten Dunst, tensions arise between Phil and his new sister-in-law. Phil's cruelty and manipulation intensify as he tries to maintain control over the ranch and his own insecurities and repressed homosexual desires. The arrival of Rose's frail, effeminate son Peter, played by Kodi Smit-McPhee, further complicates matters, as he forms a bond with Rose that threatens Phil's dominance. Initially bullied by Phil, he eventually forms a homoerotic bond with the older man before murdering him by infecting him with anthrax from an infected steer.

Film theorist Patricia White considers Campion along with Chloé Zhao (the last woman before her to win an Oscar for Best Director, and one of only three along with Campion and Kathryn Bigelow) and Kelly Reichardt and writes about all three female directors that "By messing with the Western, these women directors are taking on the masculinist presumptions of auteur criticism in other ways as well."[25] What the three have in common, according to White, is that they "all reference genre to question the masculinist Western ideology of rugged individualism, even as they use these works to distinguish themselves as individuals within the cinematic marketplace of auteurism."[26] Certainly this is true of *The Power of the Dog*, a film drenched in the ethos of tough men and women trying to rebuild the trappings of civilization in the rustic but beautiful wilds. Nevertheless, important differences remain. As White points out, "Where Reichardt and Zhao favor realism over iconography to register the force exercised by the settler colonial past on a quotidian neoliberal present, Campion pulls in the opposite direction: toward melodrama."[27]

Indeed, it is here, at the marriage of melodrama and the rugged, masculinist genre par excellence of the Western, that Campion leaves her mark and makes her most explicit philosophical intervention into what we might call, with the Italian philosopher Gianni Vattimo, her own version of the power of *weak thought*. As the philosopher responded to the question posed of whether we can conceive of a rather paradoxically sounding "strong weak thought":

> I believe that we may. In a strong theory of weakness, the philosopher's role would not derive from the world "as it is," but from the world viewed as the product of a history of interpretation throughout the history of human cultures. This philosophical effort would focus on interpretation as a process of weakening, a process in which the weight of objective structures is reduced.[28]

It is precisely insofar as Campion's film reveals the patriarchal structures of domination and violence that characterize the most iconic of American genres as the product of a specific history of interpretation, and one that could be seen otherwise, with other kinds of heroes and villains that her film functions to redefine the implicit gender expectations of the Western genre turning it into a "strong weak Western."

So, what does it mean that Campion has made a Western and does it matter? Patricia White, who discusses the interesting trend of revisionist

Westerns by female filmmakers from Reichardt's *First Cow* to Zhao's *The Rider*, and *Nomadland*, as well as *The Power of the Dog*, could not say it better: "By messing with the Western, these women directors are taking on the masculinist presumptions of auteur criticism in other ways."[29] One of the key revisions, one of the principal "other ways" to approach such masculinist presumptions, has to do with weapons. Jean-Luc Godard famously said, "All you need to make a movie is a girl and a gun," supposedly capturing the essence of his minimalist and provocative approach to filmmaking by emphasizing the fundamental elements of drama, action, and intrigue, but at the same time revealing the masculinist auteur centrality of sexualized female bodies and weaponized violence. In Campion's Western, in stark contrast, it is the male body that is sexualized, and the violence takes place without guns, becoming a cinematic expression of "weak thought."

It has been widely noted that tenderness, queer desire, and misogynistic brutality amplify each other in *The Power of the Dog*. In her onstage interview after the film's opening at the New York Film Festival, Campion introduced Ari Wegner, the female DOP of *The Power of the Dog*, with these words: "I felt like this is a very masculine story and I don't want to abandon all the ladies and so I thought I could have a female DOP and wouldn't it be brilliant if it could be Ari?"[30] The two further talk about the task of developing a language for the film together and how the visuals became embedded in the themes of the story. To the specific point of a feminist cinematic approach, Wegner talks about the non-use of weapons on the screen. In fact, there are no classic Western weapons shown in *The Power of the Dog*, ever. The brutality, Wegner says, was expressed in other ways. In an interview in the *LA Times*, Wegner says about the lack of guns, "I never thought of it as a western when we were shooting it, though it has all the classic, western elements. Everything, that is, except guns." As she adds, "For us, the danger was already in the house. There's no need to pull a gun out in order to terrify someone and keep them psychologically immobilized."[31]

It's hard to overestimate the impact on a genre like the Western of intentionally robbing it of its most iconic prop. And in Campion's case, the absence of guns acts like an intensifier of all the other iconic elements of a Western masterpiece: glorious big-sky scenery, horses and steer, cowboys and hats, good and evil, and the ever-present menace of violence. Of course, she is not the only director to have undermined this genre. Sergio Leone was perhaps the first to see the potential fodder for an auteur's approach to reinventing a cinematic universe inside the Western.

Such reinvention takes place already at the level of locations. In Sergio Leone's classic Spaghetti Western *Once Upon a Time in the West*, locations of Navajo reservations in Arizona and Utah were mixed in with images produced in *Cinecittà* studios in Rome. Internationally recognized American actors (Charles Bronson, Henry Ford, and others), as well as Italian film stars (Claudia Cardinale), were brought together to create and inhabit an imperial-colonial film space, a European construction of North America that is driven by an Americanism that Nietzsche called "the true vice of the new world."[32] In his Spaghetti Westerns, Sergio Leone, who coincidentally, just like Jane Campion, was also the son of a film actress and a director, in his case Vincenzo Leone, a Napolitano silent film era director, used an "international cast, multilingual personnel, dubbing, and locations all set all over the world."[33] Campion's internationalism for her Western was to film it in New

Zealand, although the novel on which it is based is set in Montana. Her cast was equally international and renowned, as was the case of the Spaghetti Westerns.

In her reading, White draws a connection between the main character Phil's homoerotic desire as a reaction or answer to the "toxic masculinity" (a phrase that Campion herself has used in a press conference albeit apologizing for its cliche) of the 2016 Trump era during which she read Thomas Savage's original novel (1967). Just as "Elsaesser linked the tortured, inarticulate, repressed families of 1950s melodramas of the 1950s to the Eisenhower years in American and Cold War hysteria"—as White has it.[34] However, in Campion's case, it is her "fascination with the homoerotic desire at the heart of Savage's novel [that] allows her to recuperate its protagonist," because in Phil's case, his "tough performance of masculinity conceals a sensitive soul and tender touch."[35]

This seemingly paradoxical conflict between inner and outer natures emerges in Jordan Kisner's profile of Campion for *The New York Times Magazine*. As Kisner writes,

> She had been showing me photos of a few of the marble Rodin sculptures she admired, and she pulled me over to look at a few similar pieces on display nearby. She preferred them to the big bronze casts. They were of children's faces, or women, emerging from the stone with a hazy, dreamlike quality. These pieces were so different from Rodin's more famous sculptures of men, in which every muscle and vein was articulated. It was incredible, she thought, taking more pictures, how you could get that kind of softness out of marble.[36]

In the case of *The Power of the Dog*, that Rodin bronze makes its appearance in Benedict Cumberbatch's extraordinary turn as Phil Burbank, the tough-as-nails rancher whose tender, queer soul is buried beneath layers of rock-hard, exquisitely sculpted marble.

Tenderness, Kisner adds, "may not be the first thing you see in a Campion film, but it is fundamentally what she's painting with." The author goes on to remind us how the quality underlies so many of the film's characters, whatever the exterior. And the exterior is grim indeed: "the castration, the cruelty, the extremity of suffering." Under these, though, tenderness pokes up like crocuses in a fragile spring:

> But there's also the gentle way a teenage boy's hands shape the paper flowers he likes to make; Dunst's trembling lip and the soft way she dances with her husband in the sunset on the day of their marriage; the nakedly sensual, gentle scene of Phil lying in the tall grass, communing with a lost lover by trailing the dead man's scarf so that it caresses his face and body; the way he begins to make room for the boy whose paper flowers he mocked. Where there is tenderness, something is unguarded. Tenderness invites a moment of suspense: Care or real hurt can happen next. Campion's gift is showing the chaotic mix of wounding and care in human activity, and how the terrifying moment of being opened to both possibilities is an experience of the sublime.[37]

One of her most striking redefining moves is how Campion makes the hidden tenderness of queer desire the core of her melodrama.[38] However, unlike in *Brokeback Mountain* (2005), where queer love is requited even while persecuted, finding its expression out in the wilds of the West, away from social opprobrium, *The Power of the Dog* presents a further twist, a redefining gaze of the second order. At the end of the film we find out that Phil Burbank's menacing, brute masculinity hides the softer soul of a younger man who was a scholar of classical literature, and who had been the lover of his older mentor, Bronco Henry.

The film's cameras turn Phil's moments of erotic recollection into occasions to redefine the traditionally female role as the object of the erotic gaze into a male one. We see Phil undressing in the wilderness and caressing his body with a scarf; we see him bathing nude. And into the camera's gaze steps Rose's effeminate son, Peter. The scene is crucial enough that it merits a closer analysis. Phil Burbank rides his horse through the woods near a river, observing other cowboys bathing naked and frolicking with each other (1:10:45). The camera mimics his gaze, suggesting a voyeuristic perspective. Slowly moving along the river, the POV hides behind trees and plants, focusing on the men. This shot evokes a sense of illicit observation, with the audience positioned as mere watchers, absent from the action. The scene carries a clear sexual undertone; the naked men are secretly watched, hinting at forbidden desires. Earlier, Phil had meticulously shined the saddle of his late friend and lover, implying Phil's lingering affection and obsession. The fetishization of leather symbolizes homosexual longing, establishing Campion's narrative of queer desire.

Phil carries a piece of cloth to the river, linking this scene to the earlier one and reinforcing the theme of hidden desires. Filmed frontally but from behind, Phil appears secretive (1:11:42). He undresses slowly, accompanied by uneasy music that heightens the tension. The viewer experiences the discomfort of witnessing something taboo. Phil kneels in the grass, shirtless, and begins to open his pants (1:12:01) (Figure 45).

FIGURE 45 The Power of the Dog, *2021*.

The music intensifies, amplifying the tension that begs for release, yet remains unresolved. This sexual tension revolves around the piece of cloth Phil brought, now carefully extracted from his crotch. The prolonged frontal shot, despite its duration, keeps the viewer aware of the camera's presence, enhancing the uneasy atmosphere. It hints at the revelation of Phil's hidden truth: Bronco Henry was more than a friend.

When Phil discovers he is being observed, he chases Peter away in anger, and for a while, his homophobic abuse of the boy continues. But he also begins to see his younger self in the young man and eventually appears to want to mentor him the same way of his own mentor and lover. Here, then, is where Campion's second redefining twist enters the picture. Phil teaches the younger man to cut and dry rawhide and weave it into a whip. Knowing that Phil is working on making him such a whip as a gift, Peter offers him strips of hide he has cut from a cow they found together earlier and that had died from anthrax. After Phil dies an agonizing death from anthrax, with which he has been contaminated purposefully by Peter, we see Peter opening a Bible and reading a verse from Psalm 22 in *The Book of Common Prayer*: "O you my help, come quickly to my aid! Deliver my soul from the sword, my precious life from the power of the dog!" The referent of the last clause in the film is necessarily ambiguous—who is the dog whose power we fear and from which we pray for deliverance?

In her profile of Campion, Kisner relates how the director turned to meditation to become more relaxed and led in inspiration, and how during writing *The Power of the Dog*, Campion even used the help of a dream-interpreter to allow the story to emerge, which she revealed during an interview at the opening of the film at the New York Film Festival. At that same opening, Campion also revealed further that, during her childhood, she and her sister had a babysitter who was abusive and played cruel games with them. The story she shared was that the two of them, when they were about five and seven respectively, tried to reveal the abuse to the parents. Jane did not have the courage to talk about it and sent her older sister Anna by herself. They didn't get the result they wanted, however. The parents did not let the babysitter go.

This anecdote reveals something about the nature of power in the film's title, and what may inform the special twist that Campion brings to the Western—specifically, how the weak and powerless may accrue to themselves their own, at times invisible but for that very reason dangerous, power. As Patricia White, along with others such as Manohla Dargis,[39] has noted, there is a distinct resemblance between Peter and Norman Bates "as played by the similarly sad young man Anthony Perkins in Alfred Hitchcock's *Psycho*." It's also been noted critically, White continues, that like Hitchcock's take on the murderous Bates, "Campion leans into homophobic codes in the execution of

Peter's plot to protect his mother."[40] Nevertheless, White goes on to argue, Campion's direction—from the camera's identification with Peter's gaze to the almost lascivious interest in the men's fingers as they stretch and twist rawhide strips into the braided whip—clearly works to create an identification with Peter.

Peter's sly smile indicates he has stepped into the role of help and has delivered his mother and himself from Phil's power. But it could also be read, and this I think is the point of Campion's interpretation, as meaning that Peter has assumed that power in a narrative twist toward a kind of final "reparational justice" and liberation as we have seen in *The Piano*. Let's return to the complaint in Ps. 22:19-22 that the book's title and story are based on:

> But You, O LORD, do not be far from Me; O My Strength, hasten to help Me! Deliver Me from the sword, My precious life from the power of the dog. Save Me from the lion's mouth And from the horns of the wild oxen! You have answered Me.[41]

This complaint to be freed from the "power of the dog" and from "the lion's mouth" could also be Phil's last cry for his soul to be delivered from Peter's power. Peter, cast aside as a dog, belittled and abused, has assumed the power of the abjected, of the ignored. The power that comes to those who are systematically underestimated. For it is from his very bookishness, his study of medicine, his ability to apprentice himself and learn from those around him, including Phil, that his power comes. His is the power of the weak, a power in the face of which we may witness the weight of objective structure, like that of the patriarchy, of the power of tough, manly men, weaken and ultimately wear away.

The Redefining Gaze

In this chapter, we saw Campion redefining three genres, melding them into her own auteurship: the genre of the noir thriller *In the Cut*, the genre of the detective series *Top of the Lake*, and the Western genre of *The Power of the Dog*. In all three genres, Campion again creates a female and, in the last case, a queer gaze, opening up both a female and queer interiority, as all films and series in question explore the premises of male violence. The outcome is the laying bare of a cinematic vulnerability to the condition of those without power, to say it with her last film. While *In the Cut* shows this vulnerability through the obfuscated gaze as a memento mori of the precarious state of femininity that is always destined to death and whose masochistic scars have been "self-inflicted" by a patriarchal gaze that imagines women's bodies as always already cut up, the theme of women's vulnerability is also driving the story of Campion's redefining of the TV detective genre in *Top of the Lake*. Robin Griffin, who had been gang-raped as a teenager, which led to pregnancy, had to give her baby up for adoption, offering us a glimpse into the ambiguous state of mind of the sexual assault survivor turned detective and redeemer. In both of these films, a redefining gaze onto women's vulnerability and "disarticulation" emerges into an exploration of what it might be like to "be in the cut."

Dana Polan commented on *In the Cut* before its release with the following interesting speculation:

> It is easy to imagine that, if produced, In the Cut will be judged to a large degree in terms of its relation of what people have

> come to expect from Jane Campion as a director. That is, it may be read either as a film that extends the realm of feminist desire in new directions and opens up bold possibilities for women' self determination or as one that beneath its chic eroticism replays old stories of female masochism.[42]

It will take Campion until the release of *The Power of the Dog* to be able to fully escape this ambiguous female space of being "in the cut" with her redefinition of the genre of the traditional Western and the opening of the "cut" of *male* vulnerability. In *The Power of the Dog*, Campion investigates, for the first time in depth and with fullest empathy, male repressed sexuality and the nature of unfulfilled and unacknowledged homoerotic desire. This leads to not only a "revisionist western," but also to a "lament for the limits the world puts on us and those we shoulder until we can no longer bear them."[43] As said earlier, this power comes to those who have been systematically underestimated, like Peter, and to say it with Dargis, "And while it is a tragedy, it is also a liberation story." This might be another reason for *The Power of the Dog*'s success, since like *The Piano*, it offers us a glimpse of the outside of the complex and at times fatal entanglement between our desires and our possibilities in the real world. What both films have in common is that through revenge narratives they leave viewers with a sense of empowerment.

5

Conclusion

Jane Campion and the Twenty-First-Century Revolution of Female Auteurship

Throughout these past chapters, I've tried to show that Jane Campion is not only a feminist auteur but also how she paved the way for a revolution of female auteurship in the twenty-first century. In 2018, Campion revealed that for women directors from her generation, the #MeToo and #TimesUp movements served a key role in making the world aware of the hardship that women had in the field of film directing and writing. Campion compared this important moment of the #MeToo era, which revealed to the world that abuse had been at the core of their experiences in many professional fields, to the Berlin Wall coming down: "I think we have lived in one of the more ferocious patriarchal periods of our time, the '80s, '90s, and noughties. Capitalism is such a macho force. I felt run over."[1] It has taken Campion half a century of filmmaking to be able to be seen and accepted as a "feminist filmmaker," a term she now owns, as we will see in the below examples.

It is obvious that for forerunners in any field, the success rate is particularly low, as there aren't any role models the pioneers can look up to. What is more, many pioneers don't want to look back but rather look forward toward an unknown future. From my own experience directing *The Conductor*,[2] a documentary about the life experience of the first woman to head an A-level symphony orchestra in the United States, I learned that my protagonist, Marin Alsop, did not look back at her many rejections but instead created the opportunities she never had for women conductors of the next generations, for whom she has created a fellowship program[3]: "You have to be able to fail massively, and completely, because otherwise you will only ever play it safe."[4] This statement definitely could be applied to Jane Campion, who took the risk of succeeding and failing in the box office, and of overcoming or ignoring a certain kind of film critic who feels at ease doubting her abilities as a female auteur.[5] Having to deal with the continued questioning of her abilities or even existence also rings true in some mainstream media outlets such as the Swiss Cineman magazine, where in a recent list of the "best women auteurs," Jane Campion was not mentioned, while Greta Gerwig and Chloé Zhao were listed as the two top female directors one has to keep an eye on.[6] Everybody forgets the forerunners and the hard work they have done. This is why I want to recall Jane Campion and Greta Gerwig honoring the Italian forerunner Lina Wertmüller at the 2019 Governor's Awards, which I already discussed in Chapter 1. As a combined force of two powerful and critically acclaimed female directors, Campion and Gerwig teamed up to give a speech in tandem, remembering and honoring Wertmüller, the first woman to have ever been nominated for an Oscar for her *Pasqualino Settebellezze*. As we can see in the hand-gesture below in Figure 46, Campion compares the 5 total nominations for women directors with the 350 nominations and seventy awards for male directors while commenting on the "staggering inequality," as I have already mentioned in Chapter 1.

In the meantime, since these Governor's Awards, Greta Gerwig made *Barbie*, an adaptation of a twentieth-century doll icon, which has a certain resemblance with *Pasqualino*, in its transgressiveness and craziness. As Gerwig herself says, comparing her film to *Pasqualino*, "it had to be totally bananas."[7] *Barbie* made $162 million the first weekend it came out, and $500 million during the first 10 days of its release. While it can be contested if *Barbie* could be called a truly feminist film (not least since it was financed by the manufacturer of Barbie itself), the film did put a woman director at the forefront of

FIGURE 46 *Greta Gerwig and Jane Campion at the Lina Wertmüller Lifetime Awards.*

Hollywood, and this, for Campion, is a reason to celebrate. While I don't want to dive into the pros and cons of *Barbie* itself, I do want to mention that no other female director before Gerwig had ever made that much money with a film.

It is no surprise that Campion would love *Barbie*, a film that takes the Barbie doll apart and fragments it into pieces in a completely surprising and new way, thematizing in a particularly funny scene on the lack of a vagina. In Campion's televised conversation with Greta Gerwig and Noah Baumbach at the WB Awards[8] about their film's success, she emphasizes her admiration for "turning Barbie, a feminist icon, on its head." Campion shares with the writer-director couple that she herself wasn't allowed to play with Barbie dolls, just like Greta Gerwig, and in this refreshingly frank interview, the two women agree that this doll icon was a site of many frustrations. Campion, who in this interview appears like a mentor to Gerwig ("Greta, I am proud of you"), says that she was jealous that Greta Gerwig was able to create something so "funny and beloved." In *A Girl's Own Story*, Campion showed her own take on the Barbie doll in the girl's bedroom, where Pam keeps her dolls on a shelve, which at the time of that film in the early eighties was far from representing an icon of liberation and empowerment, but rather a symbol of female anxiety and horror of not being "good enough." It took another half a century for this iconic doll to be liberated by Gerwig in her film *Barbie*, where the doll manages to escape her own beauty myth of female perfection, heteronormativity, and white supremacy (Figure 47).

As has been pointed out by so many film critics, and most recently by Jordan Kisner, Campion's films are filled with so many metaphors, allegories, myths, and dream-like structures that they form their own

FIGURE 47 A Girl's Own Story, *1984.*

semiotic system. Here are some of the key creative preoccupations for Campion as a filmmaker: "the feminine confronting the masculine; the use of landscape to evoke psychological states; mothers and daughters; family units struggling with feelings of love; alienation and betrayal."[9] All of her films share the exploration of the inner lives of "traumatized heroines in confrontation with terror."[10] Her interest in those living at the margins took on a new face with *The Power of the Dog*, as discussed in Chapter 4. In an interview quoted in Kisner's article, she reveals that her interest in that film as a director was the exploration of what humans are like as *wild creatures* and as distinct from what society wants them to turn them into.

This leads me to my final point about what Campion can teach us as a feminist director. In her interview with Gerwig and Baumbach about their film *Barbie*, she talks about the fact that, for her, directing is about creating a tone and holding it. In order to find the tone,

Campion uses all sorts of methods from meditation to making sure she gets enough sleep. She is also known to have used a dream analyst and shamans to help her understand this "tone." Her primary job as a director, as she discusses with Kisner, is to listen to the actors and to observe and see them: "You're creating a situation where they feel relaxed and confident that you are with them, that you're never going to judge them or go against. You'll just try in every way to help."[11]

This closeness to her characters is also something that, for instance, Benedict Cumberbatch for his role as Phil Burbank, admits was closer than any other director he had ever worked with. Working with Nicole Kidman on *The Portrait of a Lady*, Campion is shown in the behind-the-scenes documentary soothing the crying actress in a motherly and caring way. Being in such close touch with her characters is how Campion is able to judge whether a scene that they are performing or acting out *feels* right to her and whether it can hold that tone and the intention that she feels inside of her. The next question Campion asks and that derives from this inner voice she is following is, how can she extend this vision to the other crew members such as her producer, production designer, or director of photography. In order to communicate with these people, she draws her own storyboard so she can own the scene and her vision and share it with her team.

But how do we get close to Campion's characters when we just see them on the big screen? I want to end with a very short case study from her film *Bright Star* (2009). While I wasn't able to discuss *Bright Star* in detail in this book, I want to include a visual example of the film's storytelling and editing technique to demonstrate how Campion was able to bring her two main characters close to the viewer's hearts. *Bright Star* tells the story of the last three years of the poet John Keats and is set in the eighteenth century, like her other historical dramas, *The Piano* and *The Portrait of a Lady*. Fanny Brawne, played by Abbie Cornish, is a young woman fashionista of her time who creates dresses, hats, and various other garments for balls, and who falls in love with the famous poet who later dies prematurely of tuberculosis. As Campion reports about the interaction between the actors, the tension between them was so strong that oftentimes they did not even have to *do* or *say* anything to build a powerful atmosphere in the scene. In the below sequence, we see Fanny running away in desperation after finding out about her lover's death (Figure 48). While the first shot tells the story of her being lost without him, looking like a little tree in the wide field, the subsequent shot that changes the scale of the figure dramatically brings her close to our hearts (Figure 49). In other words, the wide shot created the necessary tension and expectation for the medium shot that surprises us by its change of scale and throws us into Fanny's tender grief. Campion approaches her characters' moods with precision and gracious tenderness. This tenderness arises from

FIGURE 48 Bright Star *(2009).*

FIGURE 49 Bright Star ***(2009).***

the vulnerability that is laid bare and made accessible in all of her characters as something to be shared, as something natural that we don't need to hide from.

I want to end on this note of changing scales and sizes. As mentioned in Chapter 1, Campion admires Rodin and his sculptures. It is precisely her ability to work with these "hard materials"—traumatic transgression, sexual repression, and power abuse—that brings out the "figure" or "human form" in the marble. She is like Rodin, but in her case, she gets the softness out of the marble by her sheer imagination and by applying her feminist lens.

I would like to conclude my examination of Jane Campion's film work by returning to Randall Halle's framework, introduced in Chapter 1, to reiterate that the *visual alterity* with which Campion transgresses, sexualizes, and redefines genres for the female lived experiences of her characters on-screen is, by any definition worth the label, profoundly feminist.

NOTES

Chapter 1

1 See Rosalind Galt and Karl Schnoover, "Introduction: The Impurity of Art Cinema," in *Global Art Cinema: New Theories and Histories*, ed. Rosalind Galt and Kar Schoonover (Oxford: Oxford University Press, 2010), 3–27.

2 Patricia White, *Women's Cinema, World Cinema: Projecting Contemporary Feminisms* (Durham, NC: Duke University Press, 2015), 4 and 29.

3 White, *Women's Cinema*, 31–2

4 "Chacun son cinéma; ou, Ce petit coup au coeur quand la lumière s'éteint et que le film commence" ("To each his or her own cinema, or the little shock to the heart when the light turns off and the movie starts"), *Festival de Cannes*, 2007, https://www.festival-cannes.com/en/festival/films/chacun-son-cinema#:~:text=Synopsis,film%20lovers%20the%20world%20over.

5 White, *Women's Cinema*, 32.

6 See the "Press Conference of the Feature Films," at "Press Conference—Jane Campion: 'I feel free to make the right decision. We'll vote for our favorite film . . . ,'" *Festival de Cannes*, May 14, 2014, https://www.festival-cannes.com/en/75-editions/retrospective/2014/actualites/articles/press-conference-jane-campion-i-feel-free-to-make-the-right-decision-we-ll-vote-for-our-favourite-film.

7 Kennedy Fraser, "Portrait of the Director," *Vogue* 187, no. 1 (1997): 144–9, 149.

8 The US distributor and fiscal sponsor Women Make Movies, founded in 1977, is still today the largest distributor of films by and about women and is the US distributor of Campion's early films *A Girl's Own Story*, *Passionless Moment*s and *Peel*.

9 Mary Cantwell, "Jane Campion's Lunatic Women," *New York Times*, September 19, 1993, https://www.nytimes.com/1993/09/19/magazine/jane-campion-s-lunatic-women.html.

10 Sue Thornham, "Starting To Feel Like A Chick," *Feminist Media Studies* 7, no. 1 (2007): 33–46, 44.

11 Alison Butler, *Women's Cinema: The Contested Screen* (London: Wallflower, 2022), 61, italics original.

12 White, *Women's Cinema*, 33.

13 Geetha Ramanathan, *Feminist Auteurs: Reading Women's Films* (London: Wallflower, 2006).

14 Laura Mulvey, "Visual Pleasure and Narrative Cinema," *Screen* 16, no. 3 (1975): 6–18, 11.

15 Luce Irigaray, *This Sex which Is Not One*, trans. Catherine Porter and Carolyn Burke (Ithaca, NY: Cornell University Press, 1985).

16 Charlotte Brunsdon, "General Introduction," in *Films for Women*, ed. Charlotte Brunsdon (London: British Film Institute, 1986), 1–6, 3. See also Hilary Radner, "'In Extremis': Jane Campion and the Woman's Film," in *Jane Campion: Cinema, Nation, Identity*, ed. Hilary Radner, Alistair Fox, and Irène Bessière (Detroit, MI: Wayne State University Press, 2009), 3–26.

17 Jami Bernard, *Chick Flicks: A Movie Lover's Guide to the Movies Women Love* (Seacaucus: Carol, 1996), vii and 17.

18 White, *Women's Cinema*, 34.

19 bell hooks, *Outlaw Culture: Resisting Representations* (New York: Routledge, 1994), 141.

20 White, *Women's Cinema*, 35.

21 White, *Women's Cinema*, 34.

22 Mark Stiles, "Jane Campion," in *Jane Campion: Interviews*, ed. Virginia Wright Wexman (Jackson: University Press of Mississippi, 1999), 3–8, 6–7.

23 See Julie Beruccelli, dir., *Jane Campion: la femme cinéma* (Films du Poisson, 2022).

24 Bernadette Wegenstein, dir., *The Conductor* (Waystone, 2021).

25 See Christine Kearney, "Filmmaker Jane Campion's Biggest Fan? Tarantino," *Reuters*, September 16, 2009, https://www.reuters.com/article/us-campion/filmmaker-jane-campions-biggest-fan-tarantino-idINTRE58F69Y20090916.

26 Bertuccelli, *Jane Campion*.

27 Bertuccelli, *Jane Campion.*

28 Bertuccelli, *Jane Campion.*

29 Bertuccelli, *Jane Campion.*

30 Kristen Williamson, "The New Filmmakers," in Wexman, *Jane Campion: Interviews*, 9–10, 10.

31 Cantwell, "Jane Campion's Lunatic Women."

32 Marli Feldvoss, "Jane Campion: Making Friends by Directing Films," trans. Andrea Reimann, in Wexman, *Jane Campion: Interviews*, 96–100, 98.

33 "Greta Gerwig and Jane Campion Honor Lina Wertmüller at the 2019 Governors Awards," *YouTube*, uploaded by Oscars, October 28, 2019, 2:15–2:31, https://youtu.be/AcaTL9oGahU.

34 "Greta Gerwig," 3:10–3:11.

35 "Greta Gerwig," 3:13–3:22.

36 "Greta Gerwig," 3:32–3:36.

37 Kathleen McHugh, *Jane Campion* (Urbana and Chicago, IL: University of Illinois Press, 2007), 3.

38 "Portrait of a Woman," *Mail & Guardian*, March 14, 1997: https://mg.co.za/article/1997-03-14-portrait-of-a-woman/.

39 Alistair Fox, *Jane Campion. Authorship and Personal Cinema* (Bloomington, IN: Indiana University Press, 2011), 140.

40 Stiles, "Jane Campion," 3. See also Carrie Rickey, "A Director Strikes an Intimate Chord," in Wexman, *Jane Campion: Interviews*, 50–3, 52: "I realized I was trying to storytell, and perhaps I should do the storytelling more directly."

41 Radner, "'In Extremis': Jane Campion and the Woman's Film," 14.

42 Ryan Uytdewilligen, "What Is Auteur Theory in Filmmaking?," *InFocus Film School*, November 5, 2019, https://infocusfilmschool.com/auteur-theory-director-filmmakers.

43 Kaja Silverman, *The Acoustic Mirror. The Female Voice in Psychoanalysis and Cinema* (Bloomington, IN and Indianapolis: Indiana University Press, 1988), 194. I will come back to Silverman's argument in more detail in Chapter 2.

44 Andrew Sarris, "Notes on the Auteur Theory in 1962," in *Auteurs and Authorship: A Film Reader*, ed. Barry Keith Grant (Malden: Blackwell, 2008), 35–45, 45.

45 Patricia White, "Women Auteurs, Western Promises," *Film Quarterly* 75, no. 4 (2022): 23–33, 29.

46 Jordan Kisner, "Inside Jane Campion's Cinema of Tenderness and Brutality," *New York Times*, November 16, 2021, https://www.nytimes.com/2021/11/16/magazine/jane-campion-power-of-the-dog.html.

47 Bertuccelli, *Jane Campion*. See also Kim Hill, "Dame Jane Campion: The Power of the Filmmaker," *RNZ*, November 13, 2021, https://www.rnz.co.nz/national/programmes/saturday/audio/2018820385/dame-jane-campion-the-power-of-the-filmmaker; and Marriska Fernandes, "'This is the Most Empowering Time': Jane Campion, 67, on Aging in Hollywood and Her New Film, 'The Power of the Dog,'" *Everything Zoomer*, December 1, 2021, https://www.everythingzoomer.com/arts-entertainment/2021/12/01/jane-campion-aging-in-hollywood-the-power-of-the-dog.

48 White, *Women's Cinema*, 30.

49 Bertuccelli, *Jane Campion*.

50 Maria Tatar, *The Heroine with 1,001 Faces* (New York: Norton, 2021), 9.

51 Vincent Ostria and Thierry Jousse, "The Piano: Interview with Jane Campion," trans. Michele Curley, in Wexman, *Jane Campion: Interviews*, 124–32, 129.

52 Fox, *Jane Campion*.

53 Bertuccelli, *Jane Campion*.

54 Bertuccelli, *Jane Campion*.

55 Randall Halle, *Visual Alterity: Seeing Difference in Cinema* (Urbana, IL: University of Illinois Press, 2021), 3.

56 See Gilles Deleuze, *Cinema 1: The Movement-Image*, trans. Hugh Tomlinson and Barbara Habberjam (Minneapolis: University of Minnesota Press, 1986); Gilles Deleuze, *Cinema 2: The Time-Image*, trans. Hugh Tomlinson and Robert Galeta (Minneapolis: University of Minnesota Press, 1989); Jean Epstein, *Critical Essays and New Translations*, ed. Sarah Keller and Jason N. Paul (Amsterdam: Amsterdam University Press, 2012); Maurice Merleau-Ponty, *Sense and Non-Sense: Studies in Phenomenology and Existential Philosophy*, trans. Hubert L. Dreyfus and Patricia Allen Dreyfus (Evanston:

Northwestern University Press, 1992), 48–59; and Edmund Husserl, *Phantasy, Image Consciousness, and Memory (1898–1925)*, ed. Rudolf Bernet (Cham: Springer, 2005).

57 Halle, *Visual Alterity*, 5.

58 Halle, *Visual Alterity*, 11–12.

59 "Passionless Moments," *Ozmovies*, https://www.ozmovies.com.au/movie/passionless-moments.

60 Michel Ciment, "Interviews with Jane Campion," in McHugh, *Jane Campion*, 147–54, 149. See also Ben Kooyman, "Work-for-Hire Juvenilia: After Hours (Jane Campion, 1984)," *CTEQ Annotations on Film* 84 (2017), https://www.sensesofcinema.com/2017/cteq/after-hours-2.

61 Bertuccelli, *Jane Campion*.

62 Bertuccelli, *Jane Campion*.

63 Deb Verhoeven, *Jane Campion* (New York: Routledge, 2005), 186.

64 See Andrew L. Urban, "The Contradictions of Jane Campion, Cannes Winner," in Wexman, *Jane Campion: Interviews*, 14–15, 15.

65 See Wexman, *Jane Campion: Interviews*, xv; and Maitland McDonagh, "Jane Campion's 'Angel' Is Another Quirky Soul," *New York Times*, May 19, 1991, https://www.nytimes.com/1991/05/19/archives/film-jane-campions-angel-is-another-quirky-soul.html.

66 Gwendolyn Audrey Foster, "Girlhood in ReverseJane Campion's 2 Friends (1986)," *CTEQ Annotations on Film* 84 (2017), https://www.sensesofcinema.com/2017/cteq/2-friends.

67 Philippa Hawker, "Jane Campion," in Wexman, *Jane Campion: Interviews*, 20–5, 21.

68 Thomas Bourguignon and Michel Ciment, "Interview with Jane Campion: More Barbarian than Aesthete," trans. Michele Curley, in Wexman, *Jane Campion: Interviews*, 101–12, 110.

69 Katherine Tulich, "Jane's Film Career Takes Wing," in Wexman, *Jane Campion: Interviews*, 71–3, 73.

70 Hunter Cordaiy, "Jane Campion Interviewed," in Wexman, *Jane Campion: Interviews*, 74–82, 77.

71 Radner, "'In Extremis': Jane Campion and the Woman's Film," 14.

72 White, "Women Auteurs, Western Promises," 23–33, 31–2.

73 Kisner, "Inside Jane Campion's Cinema."

74 Picnic at Hanging Rock, A film by Peter Weir, 1975, The Criterion Collection: Director approved Two-DVD Special Edition Features, 2014, Disc 2, Interview with Peter Weir (2003), 17:25-17:30.

75 See Emily Brontë, *Wuthering Heights*, ed. Ian Jack (Oxford: World's Classics, 1995), 362.

76 See Michel Ciment, "Two Interviews with Jane Campion," trans. Michele Curley, in Wexman, *Jane Campion: Interviews*, 30–44, 43.

77 See Ruth Hessey, "Campion Goes Out on a Limb—Again," in Wexman, *Jane Campion: Interviews*, 26–9, 29.

78 Kate Muir, "Jane Campion: 'Capitalism is such a macho force. I felt run over,'" *Guardian*, May 20, 2018, https://www.theguardian.com/film/2018/may/20/jane-campion-unconventional-film-maker-macho-force.

Chapter 2

1 Silverman, *The Acoustic Mirror*, 187–234.

2 Silverman, *The Acoustic Mirror*, 188.

3 Silverman, *The Acoustic Mirror*, 191.

4 Silverman, *The Acoustic Mirror*, 192.

5 Sarris, "Notes on the Auteur Theory in 1962," 538–9, quoted in Silverman, *The Acoustic Mirror*, 194.

6 Fox, *Jane Campion*, 3.

7 Fox, *Jane Campion*, 55.

8 Wexman, *Jane Campion Interviews*, XII.

9 "Portrait of a Woman."

10 Dana Polan, *Jane Campion* (London: British Film Institute, 2001), 60.

11 "God, if anyone finds out I'm in the hospital trying to make a *seven-minute* film—it's actually nine with credits—no one's ever, ever going to hire me." In: Kisner, "Inside Jane Campion's Cinema of Tenderness and Brutality."

12 Polan, *Jane Campion*, 62.

13 Fox, *Jane Campion*, 53.

14 Fox, *Jane Campion*, 54.

15 Polan, *Jane Campion*, 64.

16 Stiles, "Jane Campion,", 4–5.

17 Polan, *Jane Campion*, 71.

18 Wexman, *Jane Campion Interviews*, XV, also quoted in Fox, *Jane Campion*, 53.

19 Fox, *Jane Campion*, 56.

20 Fox, *Jane Campion*, 59.

21 Michael Renov, *The Subject of Documentary* (Minnesota: University of Minnesota Press), 2004.

22 Polan, *Jane Campion*, 79.

23 Judith Herman, *Trauma and Recovery* (Harvard, MA: Harvard University Press, 1990).

24 Ciment, "Interviews with Jane Campion," 35.

25 Alistair Fox says that in the harassment scenes in question, Lorraine "seems to be living out a fantasy of incest with a father figure at the same time that she feels abhorrence and anger at the outcome of it." *Jane Campion*, 62. While I disagree with this interpretation for this film, I will come back to this theme in the below discussion of *Holy Smoke!*.

26 Verhoeven, *Jane Campion*, 184.

27 Polan, *Jane Campion*, 81.

28 Fox, *Jane Campion*, 62.

29 Polan, *Jane Campion*, 81.

30 Ciment, "Two Interviews with Jane Campion," 38.

31 Ciment, "Two Interviews with Jane Campion," 43.

32 Interview with Donna Yuzwalk, "The Sweet Smell of Success," in Wexman, *Jane Campion Interviews*, 54.

33 Verhoeven, *Jane Campion*, 189.

34 Interview with Ruth Hessey, 1989, in Wexman, *Jane Campion Interviews*, 28.

35 Interview with Myra Forsberg, "'Sweetie' isn't Sugary," *The New York Times*, January 14, 1990.

36 Interview with Ruth Hessey, 1989, in Wexman, *Jane Campion Interviews*, 26–7.

37 Ciment, "Two Interviews with Jane Campion," 38.

38 Philip Matthews, "Leaving Sequence," *Listener* (Wellington), August 19, 1995, 45, quoted in Fox, *Jane Campion*, 72.

39 Interview with Thomas Bourguignon and Michael Ciment, "More Barbarian than Aesthete", in Wexman, *Jane Campion Interviews*, 110.

40 Fox, *Jane Campion*, 59.

41 Director's Commentary *Sweetie*.

42 "I can't work very well if I get too serious. I find seriousness very inhibiting." An interview with Lunden Barber, "Angel with An Eccentric Eye," in Wexman, *Jane Campion Interviews*, 57.

43 Fox, *Jane Campion*, 87.

44 Michel Ciment, *Jane Campion on Jane Campion* (New York: Abrams, 2023), 44.

45 Michel Ciment, *Jane Campion on Jane Campion*, (New York: Abrams Art Books, 2023), 39, 44.

46 "Portrait of a Woman."

47 Brian McFarlane, "The Portrait of a Lady," *Cinema Papers*, no. 115 (April 1998): 37.

48 Jane Campion, "Big Shell," *Rolling Stone* 426 (1988): 74–6.

49 Anna Campion and Jane Campion, *Holy Smoke. A Novel* (New York: Hyperion, 1999).

50 Ciment quoted in Fox, *Jane Campion*, 157.

51 Polan, *Jane Campion*, 142.

52 Fox, *Jane Campion*, 172.

53 Miramax press kit for *Holy Smoke*, quoted in: Fox, *Jane Campion*, 172.

54 Fox, *Jane Campion*, 158.

55 Marnie Landrot, "'La ligue des Campions': Leurs séances de travail pour l'écriture de *Holy Smoke* ont frôlé la thérapie familiale," *Télérama*, November 24, 1999, quoted in Fox: *Jane Campion*, 159.

56 https://www.nzonscreen.com/title/the-audition-1989.

57 Brett Kahr, *Sex and the Psyche: The Truth about Most Secret Fantasies* (London: Penguin, 2007).

58 Kahr, *Sex and the Psyche*, 304. quoted in Fox, *Jane Campion*, 160.

59 Polan, *Jane Campion*, 145.

60 Dion Beebe is a very wide-ranging DP who became famous for shooting Rob Marshall's *Chicago* (2002) and Michael Mann's, *Collateral* (2004). Recently, he also filmed *I Am Woman* (2019) by Unjoo Moon and the Disney production, once again directed by Rob Marshall, *The Little Mermaid* (2023).

61 Polan, *Jane Campion*, 146.

62 Polan, *Jane Campion*, 148.

63 Andrew L. Urban, "Hallucination F/X," Interview with Holy Smoke's Digital Effects Supervisor, in Urban Cinefile (quoted in Polan, *Jane Campion*, 148).

64 Dana Polan, *Jane Campion*, 155–6.

65 Monique Wittig, *One Is Not Born a Woman*, 1981, in *The Essential Feminist Reader*, ed. Estelle B. Freedman (New York: The Modern Library, 2007), 359–66. Wittig was active during the same years as Campion's early period, the 1980s.

66 Jacqueline Rose, *Sexuality in the Field of Vision* (London: Verso, 1986), 5.

67 Verhoeven, *Jane Campion*, 190.

Chapter 3

1 Rose, *Sexuality in the Field of Vision*, 7.

2 Laura Mulvey, "Visual Pleasure and Narrative Cinema," in *Feminism & Film*, ed. E. Ann Kaplan (London: Oxford University Press, 2004), 34–47 (originally published in *Screen* 16, no. 3, 1975).

3 Rose, *Sexuality in the Field of Vision*, 220.

4 I want to briefly allude here to what I have already written in the context of my introduction to my anthology *Radical Equalities and Global Feminist Filmmaking*, ed. Bernadette Wegenstein and Lauren Mushro (Wilmington, DE and Malaga, Spain: Vernon Press, 2022): It is hard to account for a feminist film history as women pioneer filmmakers have historically not been accounted for. The pioneers from the silent era have been mostly omitted from the canon of film histories, and the women filmmakers of Hollywood's classic era have been silenced. (xxiv–xxv). See also E. Ann Kaplan, "Women, Film, Resistance: Changing Paradigms," in *Women Filmmakers: Refocusing*, ed. Jacqueline Levitin, Judith Plessis, and Valerie Raoul (New York: Routledge, 2003).

5 Metz, quoted in Rose, *Sexuality in the Field of Vision*, 2.

6 Fox, *Jane Campion*, 132.

7 Polan, *Jane Campion*, 86.

8 Polan, Jane Campion, 87.

9 Polan, Jane Campion, 87.

10 Laura Mulvey, *Afterimages: On Cinema, Women, and Changing Times* (Chicago: Chicago University Press, 2019).

11 https://www.sensesofcinema.com/2017/cteq/2-friends/.

12 Michel Ciment, *Jane Campion on Jane Campion*, 39.

13 Fox, *Jane Campion*, 64.

14 Fox, *Jane Campion*, 154.

15 Polan, *Jane Campion*, 105–6.

16 Translation by Marilyn McCabe: http://numerocinqmagazine.com/2010/12/09/from-vergers-three-poems-by-rilke-translated-by-marilyn-mccabe/.

17 Fox, *Jane Campion*, 88.

18 Sue Williams, "A Light on the Dark Secrets of Depression," in *Jane Campion Interviews*, ed. Wright Wexman, 1999, 175–176.

19 Harriet Margolis, "The Campions Indulge in the Audition," in *Jane Campion: Cinema, Nation, Identity*, ed. Hilary Radner, Alistair Fox, and Irène Bessière (Detroit: MI Wayne State University Press, 2009), 39–52.

20 Alexis Brown, "An Angel at My Table (1990): Janet Frame, Jane Campion, and Authorial Control in the Auto/Biopic," *Journal of New Zealand Literature* 34, no. 1 (2016): 113–14.

21 Brown, "An Angel at My Table (1990)," 121.

22 Fox, *Jane Campion*, 93–7.

23 1996.

24 Polan, *Jane Campion*, 123.

25 Polan, *Jane Campion*, 113–15.

26 Polan, *Jane Campion*, 109.

27 Interestingly, in Campion's first version of the screenplay, Ada drowns with the piano, a less "romantic" ending and one that probably would have satisfied some of the feminist critiques of the film being too essentialist.

28 Polan, *Jane Campion*, 22; and here is the fandom website she drew from but which no longer seems active: www.fys.uio.no/magnushj/Piano/opinion.html.

29 https://www.sensesofcinema.com/2000/conference-special-effects-special-affects/fingers/.

30 Carol Jacobs, "Playing Jane Campion's Piano: Politically," *Modern Language Notes* 109, no. 5 (1994): 769.

31 Polan, *Jane Campion*, 29.

32 Cynthia Kaufman, "Colonialism, Purity, and Resistance in *The Piano*," *Socialist Review* 24, no. 1–2 (1995): 252.

33 Jaime Bihlmeyer, "Jane Campion's *The Piano*: The Female Gaze, the Speculum, and the Chora within the H(y)st(e)rical Film," *Essays in Philosophy* 4, no. 1 (2003):, 10, Article 13.

34 Robert Macklin, "Campion's Award-winning Screenplay Inspired by Novel," *Canberra Times*, April 8, 2000.

35 O-Neill Dean quoted in Fox, *Jane Campion*, 114.

36 *The Piano*, a film by Jane Campion, The Criterion Collection: Director approved 4K UHD + BluRay Special Edition Features, 2022, Audio commentary featuring a conversation between Campion and Chapman, 37: 12–38:45

37 McHugh, *Jane Campion*, 81–3.

38 *Cinema Papers*, 1993.

39 Milo Bilbrough, "The Piano," in Wexman, *Jane Campion: Interviews*, 116.

40 Fox, *Jane Campion*, 62–3.

41 Brian Stableford, *Introduction to Marguerritte, Victor, The Bacheloress* (Encino, CA: A Black Coat Press Book, 2015), 5–6.

42 Harriet Taylor Mill, "The Enfranchisement of Women," (England, 1851), in *The Essential Feminist Reader* (New York: The Modern Library, 2007), 71–2.

43 Michael Ciment, "A Voyage to Discover Herself," in Wexman, *Jane Campion Interviews*, 177.

44 Ciment, "A Voyage to Discover Herself," 180.

45 Harriet Margolis and Janet Hughes, "Jane Campion's Portrait of a Lady," in *Nineteenth-Century American Fiction on Screen*, ed. R. Barton Palmer (Cambridge: Cambridge University Press), 2007, 161.

46 Margolis and Hughes, "Jane Campion's Portrait of a Lady."

47 Michel Ciment, "Interviews with Jane Campion," in Kathleen McHugh, *Jane Campion*, 181.

48 Polan, *Jane Campion*, 127.

49 Ciment, "Interviews with Jane Campion," 179.

50 Fox, *Jane Campion*, 155.

51 Ric Gentry, "Painterly Touches" (Interview with Stuart Dryburgh), *American Cinematographer* 78, no. 1 (1997): 56.

52 Polan, *Jane Campion*, 141.

53 "Portrait of a Woman."

54 "Portrait of a Woman."

55 "Portrait of a Woman."

56 https://variety.com/1996/film/reviews/the-portrait-of-a-lady-1200446901/.

57 Fox, *Jane Campion*, 151.

Chapter 4

1 McHugh, *Jane Campion*, 123.

2 Susanna Moore, *In the Cut* (New York: Penguin Books, 1999), 19.

3 Moore, *In the Cut*, 63, 98.

4 Moore, *In the Cut*, 51. This conversation does not take place in the film version. While the film scene is misogynist in its own way, it does not even come close to the violent language of the novel.

5 Moore, *In the Cut*, 60.

6 Fox, *Jane Campion*, 179.

7 Moore, *In the Cut*, 174.

8 Moore, *In the Cut*, 78.

9 Moore, *In the Cut*, 178–9.

10 Moore, *In the Cut*, 71.

11 Jane Campion explains the use of this lens in the director's commentary to the 2004 DVD edition of the film. She adds that this kind of lens is often used in advertising.

12 Andy Klein, "Something About Frannie: Meg Ryan Finesses Her Vague Character in Jane Campion's Unimpressive 'In the Cut,'" http://www.lacitybeat.com/article.php?id=339&IssueNum=20.

13 The reason for this name change is a clearer class and race attribution. Giovanni Malloy is at least of half Italian descent. The director comments in the director's commentary: "Frannie is attracted to Malloy because he is himself. It's also a class thing."

14 One of the main causes for this ambiguity is that Malloy shares the same tattoo as the real perpetrator.

15 The novel, however, treats this narrative moment quite differently. First, it is expressed earlier that Frannie thinks Malloy is the murderer. She says to him, "I want to know what you did to her" (Moore, *In the Cut*, 152). Malloy, who does not even defend himself, starts his speech quite differently, too: "She must have been moving" (152).

16 Moore, *In the Cut*, 169.

17 In the novel, Moore alludes to the Geneva episode in a much less emphatic way, that is, in conjunction with other disappointments throughout Frannie's life, including the most recent disappointment about Malloy: "I am so ashamed by the things that used to make me unhappy. That I was upset because he lied to me about his wife and then went on vacation with her. That Yale University won't give me permission to use the letters of C.K. Whitney. That my father forgot me in Geneva." Moore, *In the Cut*, 152.

18 Campion in the DVD commentary.

19 The song was written and used in Hitchcock's 1956 *The Man Who Knew Too Much*. The verses, sung originally by Doris Day to her character's son, were rearranged for the film, as pointed out by McHugh (131).

20 The original version was written by Ray Evans for Doris Day's character Jo in Hitchcock's *The Man Who Knew Too Much* (1956), who sang the song in order to let her kidnapped son, Hank, know that she was in the same house. Besides *In the Cut*, there are many cover versions used in cinema, such as Syd Straw's version of the song in Michael Lehmann's 1989 parody of US high school life *Heathers*.

21 I would even dare to speculate that the character of Detective Robin Griffin has influenced many female detectives on television up until the most recent HBO series of *True Detective, Night Country* (2024), starring Jodie Foster in the main role.

22 Sophie Gilbert, "The Strange Confusion of *Top of the Lake: China Girl*," *The Atlantic*, September, 2017, https://www.theatlantic.com/entertainment/archive/2017/09/top-of-the-lake-china-girl-review/539367/.

23 Campion shared that she read the novel many years ago just for fun and did not think about making it into a screenplay until much later. But the story had stuck with her.

24 Mark Asquith, "Peeling the Onion of Masculinity: Jane Campion's Power of the Dog as Gothic Western," *Literature/ Film/ Quarterly* 52, no. 1, https://lfq.salisbury.edu/_issues/52_1/peeling_the_onion_of_masculinity_jane_campions_power_of_the_dog_as_a_gothic_western.html

25 White, *Women's Cinema*, 23.

26 White, *Women's Cinema*, 24.

27 White, *Women's Cinema*, 24.

28 Gianni Vattimo, Santiago Zabala, and Yaakov Mascetti, "'Weak Thought' and the Reduction of Violence: A Dialogue with Gianni Vattimo," *Common Knowledge* 8, no. 3 (Fall, 2002): 452–63, 452.

29 Patricia White, "Women Auteurs, Western Premises," *Film Quarterly* 75, no. 4: 23–33, 23.

30 https://www.youtube.com/watch?v=6CgPUPEe15E.

31 Beth Merchant, "'The Power of the Dog' is no western. Instead the camera found the delicate tensions," *The Los Angeles Times*, January 5, 2022, https://www.latimes.com/entertainment-arts/awards/story/2022-01-05/power-of-the-dog-is-no-western-instead-ari-wegner-found-the-delicate-tensions.

32 Nietzsche, *The Gay Science*, ed. Bernard Williams (Cambridge: Cambridge University Press, 2001), section 329.

33 Marcia Landy, *Cinematic Uses of the Past* (Minnesota: Minnesota Archives Edition, 2009), 185.

34 White, "Women Auteurs, Western Premises," 30.

35 Kisner, https://www.nytimes.com/2021/11/16/magazine/jane-campion-power-of-the-dog.html.

36 Kisner, https://www.nytimes.com/2021/11/16/magazine/jane-campion-power-of-the-dog.html..

37 White, *Women's Cinema*, 25.

38 Dargis, "'The Power of the Dog' Review: Wild Hearts on a Closed Frontier," *New York Times*, November. 30, 2021, https://www.nytimes.com/2021/11/30/movies/the-power-of-the-dog-review.html.

39 White, "Women Auteurs, Western Premises," 31.

40 https://www.bible.com/bible/compare/PSA.22.19-22#:~:text=Psalms%2022%3A19%2D22%20New,You%20have%20answered%20Me.

41 Polan, *Jane Campion*, 160.

42 Polan, *Jane Campion*, 160.

43 White, "Women Auteurs, Western Premises," 30.

Chapter 5

1 https://womenandhollywood.com/quote-of-the-day-jane-campion-explains-why-were-in-a-really-special-moment/.

2 https://www.theconductordoc.com/.

3 The Taki Alsop Concordia Fellowship for Women Conductors: https://takialsop.org/.

4 Marin Alsop in an interview in *The Conductor*, by Bernadette Wegenstein.

5 To give one recent example, see Sam Elliot, quoted in Joe Dolce, "1883 and The Power of the Dog: True and False in the Old West," *Quadrant Magazine*, July 16, 2022, https://quadrant.org.au/magazine/2022/07-08/1883-and-the-power-of-the-dog-true-and-false-in-the-old-west/: "What the fuck does this woman from down there know about the American west? Why the fuck did she shoot this movie in New Zealand and call it Montana?"

6 https://www.cineman.ch/article/augen-auf-diese-8-regisseurinnen-solltest-du-im-blick-behalten.

7 https://www.theguardian.com/film/2023/jul/09/it-had-to-be-totally-bananas-greta-gerwig-on-bringing-barbie-back-to-life.

8 https://www.wbawards.com/video/?film=barbie&vid=barbie_20240109_1.

9 Kisner, https://www.nytimes.com/2021/11/16/magazine/jane-campion-power-of-the-dog.html.

10 Kisner, https://www.nytimes.com/2021/11/16/magazine/jane-campion-power-of-the-dog.html.

11 Kisner, https://www.nytimes.com/2021/11/16/magazine/jane-campion-power-of-the-dog.html.

12 Fraser, "Portrait of the Director," 144–9, 149.

BIBLIOGRAPHY

Asquith, Mark. "Peeling the Onion of Masculinity: Jane Campion's Power of the Dog as Gothic Western." *Literature/ Film/ Quarterly* 52, no. 1. https://lfq.salisbury.edu/_issues/52_1/peeling_the_onion_of_masculinity_jane_campions_power_of_the_dog_as_a_gothic_western.html.

Barber, Lunden. "Angel with An Eccentric Eye." In *Jane Campion: Interviews*, edited by Virginia Wright Wexman, 57. Jackson: University Press of Mississippi, 1999.

Berger, Laura. "Quote of the Day: Jane Campion Explains Why 'We're in a Really Special Moment.'" *Women and Hollywood*, May 21, 2018. https://womenandhollywood.com/quote-of-the-day-jane-campion-explains-why-were-in-a-really-special-moment/.

Bernard, Jami. *Chick Flicks: A Movie Lover's Guide to the Movies Women Love*. Seacaucus: Carol, 1996.

Beruccelli, Julie, dir. *Jane Campion: la femme cinéma*. Films du Poisson, 2022.

Bihlmeyer, Jaime. "Jane Campion's *The Piano*: The Female Gaze, the Speculum, and the Chora within the H(y)st(e)rical Film." *Essays in Philosophy* 4, no. 1 (2003): 10, Article 13.

Bilbrough, Milo. "The Piano." In *Jane Campion: Interviews*, edited by Virginia Wright Wexman, 116. Jackson: University Press of Mississippi, 1999.

Bourguignon, Thomas and Michel Ciment. "Interview with Jane Campion: More Barbarian than Aesthete," translated by Michele Curley. In *Jane Campion: Interviews*, edited by Virginia Wright Wexman, 101–12. Jackson: University Press of Mississippi, 1999.

Brontë, Emily. *Wuthering Heights*, edited by Ian Jack. Oxford: World's Classics, 1995.

Brown, Alexis. "An Angel at My Table (1990): Janet Frame, Jane Campion, and Authorial Control in the Auto/Biopic." *Journal of New Zealand Literature* 34, no.1 (2016): 113–14.

Brunsdon, Charlotte, ed. *Films for Women*. London: British Film Institute, 1986.

Buovolo, Marisa. *Jane Campion & Ihre Filme*. Marburg: Schüren Verlag, 2024.

Butler, Alison. *Women's Cinema: The Contested Screen*. London: Wallflower, 2022.

Campion, Anna and Jane Campion. *Holy Smoke. A Novel*. New York: Hyperion, 1999.

Campion, Jane. "Big Shell." *Rolling Stone* 426 (1988): 74–6.

Cantwell, Mary. "Jane Campion's Lunatic Women." *New York Times*, September 19, 1993. https://www.nytimes.com/1993/09/19/magazine/jane-campion-s-lunatic-women.html.

Ciment, Michael. "A Voyage to Discover Herself." In *Jane Campion Interviews*, edited by Wright Wexman, 177–85. Jackson: University Press of Mississippi, 1999.

Ciment, Michel. "Two Interviews with Jane Campion," translated by Michele Curley. In *Jane Campion Interviews*, edited by Wright Wexman, 30–44. Jackson: University Press of Mississippi, 1999.

Ciment, Michel. "Interviews with Jane Campion." In *Jane Campion*, edited by Kathleen McHugh, 147–54. Urbana: University of Illinois Press, 2007.

Ciment, Michel. *Jane Campion on Jane Campion*. New York: Abrams Art Books, 2023.

Cordaiy, Hunter. "Jane Campion Interviewed." In *Jane Campion: Interviews*, edited by Virginia Wright Wexman, 74–82. Jackson: University Press of Mississippi, 1999.

Dargis, Manohla. "'The Power of the Dog' Review: Wild Hearts on a Closed Frontier." *New York Times*, November 30, 2021. https://www.nytimes.com/2021/11/30/movies/the-power-of-the-dog-review.html.

Deleuze, Gilles. *Cinema 1: The Movement-Image*, translated by Hugh Tomlinson and Barbara Habberjam. Minneapolis: University of Minnesota Press, 1986.

Deleuze, Gilles. *Cinema 2: The Time-Image*, translated by Hugh Tomlinson and Robert Galeta. Minneapolis: University of Minnesota Press, 1989.

Diekhaus, Christopher. "Augen Auf. Diese Regisseurinnen Solltest Du im Blick Behalten." *Cineman*, July 19, 2023. https://womenandhollywood.com/quote-of-the-day-jane-campion-explains-why-were-in-a-really-special-moment/.

Dolce, Joe. "1883 and The Power of the Dog: True and False in the Old West." *Quadrant Magazine,* July 16, 2022. https://quadrant.org.au/magazine/2022/07-08/1883-and-the-power-of-the-dog-true-and-false-in-the-old-west/.

Epstein, Jean. *Critical Essays and New Translations*, edited by Sarah Keller and Jason N. Paul. Amsterdam: Amsterdam University Press, 2012.

Feldvoss, Marli. "Jane Campion: Making Friends by Directing Films," translated by Andrea Reimann. In *Jane Campion: Interviews*, edited by Virginia Wright Wexman, 96–100. Jackson: University Press of Mississippi, 1999.

Fernandes, Marriska. "'This is the Most Empowering Time': Jane Campion, 67, on Aging in Hollywood and Her New Film, 'The Power of the Dog.'" *Everything Zoomer*, December 1, 2021. https://www.everythingzoomer.com/arts-entertainment/2021/12/01/jane-campion-aging-in-hollywood-the-power-of-the-dog.

Forsberg, Myra. "'Sweetie' isn't Sugary." *The New York Times*, January 14, 1990.

Foster, Gwendolyn Audrey. "Girlhood in Reverse – Jane Campion's 2 Friends (1986)." *CTEQ Annotations on Film* 84 (2017). https://www.sensesofcinema.com/2017/cteq/2-friends.

Fox, Alistair. *Jane Campion. Authorship and Personal Cinema*. Bloomington, IN: Indiana University Press, 2011.

Fraser, Kennedy. "Portrait of the Director." *Vogue* 187, no. 1 (1997): 144–9.

Galt, Rosalind and Karl Schnoover, ed. *Global Art Cinema: New Theories and Histories*. Oxford: Oxford University Press, 2010.

Gentry, Ric. "Painterly Touches" (Interview with Stuart Dryburgh). *American Cinematographer* 78, no. 1 (1997): 56.

"Greta Gerwig and Jane Campion Honor Lina Wertmüller at the 2019 Governors Awards." *YouTube*, uploaded by Oscars, October 28, 2019, 2:15–2:31. https://youtu.be/AcaTL9oGahU.

Gilbert, Sophie. "The Strange Confusion of *Top of the Lake: China Girl*." *The Atlantic*, September, 2017. https://www.theatlantic.com/entertainment/archive/2017/09/top-of-the-lake-china-girl-review/539367/.

Halle, Randall. *Visual Alterity: Seeing Difference in Cinema*. Urbana, IL: University of Illinois Press, 2021.

Hawker, Philippa. "Jane Campion." In *Jane Campion: Interviews*, edited by Virginia Wright Wexman, 20–5. Jackson: University Press of Mississippi, 1999.

Herman, Judith. *Trauma and Recovery*. Cambridge, MA: Harvard University Press, 1990.

Hessey, Ruth. "Campion Goes Out on a Limb – Again." In *Jane Campion: Interviews*, edited by Virginia Wright Wexman, 26–9. Jackson: University Press of Mississippi, 1999.

Hill, Kim. "Dame Jane Campion: The Power of the Filmmaker." *RNZ*, November 13, 2021. https://www.rnz.co.nz/national/programmes/saturday/audio/2018820385/dame-jane-campion-the-power-of-the-filmmaker.

Hooks, bell. *Outlaw Culture: Resisting Representations*. New York: Routledge, 1994.

Husserl, Edmund. *Phantasy, Image Consciousness, and Memory (1898--1925)*, edited by Rudolf Bernet. Cham: Springer, 2005.

Irigaray, Luce. *This Sex which Is Not One*, translated by Catherine Porter and Carolyn Burke. Ithaca, NY: Cornell University Press, 1985.

Jacobs, Carol. "Playing Jane Campion's Piano: Politically." *Modern Language Notes* 109, no. 5 (1994): 757–85.

Jane Campion Sits Down with writer/director Greta Gerwig and writer Noah Baumbach. https://www.wbawards.com/video/?film=barbie&vid=barbie_20240109_1.

Kahr, Brett. *Sex and the Psyche: The Truth about Most Secret Fantasies*. London: Penguin, 2007.

Kaplan, E. Ann. "Women, Film, Resistance: Changing Paradigms." In *Women Filmmakers: Refocusing*, edited by Jacqueline Levitin, Judith Plessis, and Valerie Raoul, 3–14. New York: Routledge, 2003.

Kaufman, Cynthia. "Colonialism, Purity, and Resistance in *The Piano*." *Socialist Review* 24, no. 1–2 (1995): 251.

Kearney, Christine. "Filmmaker Jane Campion's Biggest Fan? Tarantino." *Reuters*, September 16, 2009. https://www.reuters.com/article/us-campion/filmmaker-jane-campions-biggest-fan-tarantino-idINTRE58F69Y20090916.

Kisner, Jordan. "Inside Jane Campion's Cinema of Tenderness and Brutality." *New York Times*, November 16, 2021. https://www.nytimes.com/2021/11/16/magazine/jane-campion-power-of-the-dog.html.

Klein, Andy. "Something About Frannie: Meg Ryan Finesses her Vague Character in Jane Campion's Unimpressive 'In the Cut.'" http://www.lacitybeat.com/article.php?id=339&IssueNum=20.

Kooyman, Ben. "Work-for-Hire Juvenilia: After Hours (Jane Campion, 1984)." *CTEQ Annotations on Film* 84 (2017). https://www.sensesofcinema.com/2017/cteq/after-hours-2.

Landrot, Marnie. "'La ligue des Campions': Leurs séances de travail pour l'écriture de *Holy Smoke* ont frôlé la thérapie familiale." *Télérama*, November 24, 1999.

Landy, Marcia. *Cinematic Uses of the Past*. Minnesota: Minnesota Archives Edition, 2009.

Macklin, Robert. "Campion's Award-Winning Screenplay Inspired by Novel." *Canberra Times*, April 8, 2000.

Margolis, Harriet and Janet Hughes. "Jane Campion's Portrait of a Lady." In *Nineteenth-Century American Fiction on Screen*, edited by R. Barton Palmer, 161. Cambridge: Cambridge University Press, 2007.

Margolis, Harriet. "The Campions Indulge in the Audition." In *Jane Campion: Cinema, Nation, Identity*, edited by Hilary Radner, Alistair Fox, and Irène Bessière. Detroit: MI Wayne State University Press, 2009.

Matthews, Philip. "Leaving Sequence." *Listener* (Wellington), August 19, 1995.

McDonagh, Maitland. "Jane Campion's 'Angel' Is Another Quirky Soul." *New York Times*, May 19, 1991. https://www.nytimes.com/1991/05/19/archives/film-jane-campions-angel-is-another-quirky-soul.html.

McFarlane, Brian. "The Portrait of a Lady." *Cinema Papers*, no. 115, April 1998.

McHugh, Kathleen. *Jane Campion*. Urbana and Chicago, IL: University of Illinois Press, 2007.

Merchant, Beth. "'The Power of the Dog' is No Western. Instead the Camera Found the Delicate Tensions." *The Los Angeles Times*, January 5, 2022. https://www.latimes.com/entertainment-arts/awards/story/2022-01-05/power-of-the-dog-is-no-western-instead-ari-wegner-found-the-delicate-tensions.

Merleau-Ponty, Maurice. *Sense and Non-Sense: Studies in Phenomenology and Existential Philosophy*, translated by Hubert L. Dreyfus and Patricia Allen Dreyfus. Evanston: Northwestern University Press, 1992.

Mill, Harriet Taylor. "The Enfranchisement of Women." (England, 1851), In *The Essential Feminist Reader*, 71–2. New York: The Modern Library, 2007.

Moore, Susanna. *In the Cut*. New York: Penguin Books, 1999.

Moshakis, Alex. "'It Had to be Totally Bananas.' Greta Gerwig on bringing Barbie to Life." *The Guardian*, July 9, 2023. https://www.theguardian.com/film/2023/jul/09/it-had-to-be-totally-bananas-greta-gerwig-on-bringing-barbie-back-to-life.

Muir, Kate. "Jane Campion: 'Capitalism is Such a Macho Force. I Felt Run Over.'" *Guardian*, May 20, 2018. https://www.theguardian.com/film/2018/may/20/jane-campion-unconventional-film-maker-macho-force.

Mulvey, Laura. "Visual Pleasure and Narrative Cinema." *Screen* 16, no. 3 (1975): 6–18.

Mulvey, Laura. "Visual Pleasure and Narrative Cinema." In *Feminism & Film*, edited by E. Ann Kaplan. London: Oxford University Press, 2004.

Mulvey, Laura. *Afterimages: On Cinema, Women, and Changing Times*. Chicago, IL: Chicago University Press, 2019.

Nietzsche, Friedrich. *The Gay Science*, edited by Bernard Williams. Cambridge: Cambridge University Press, 2001.

Ostria, Vincent and Thierry Jousse. "The Piano: Interview with Jane Campion," translated by Michele Curley. In *Jane Campion: Interviews*, edited by Virginia Wright Wexman, 124–32. Jackson: University Press of Mississippi, 1999.

"Passionless Moments." *Ozmovies*. https://www.ozmovies.com.au/movie/passionless-moments.

Picnic at Hanging Rock, A film by Peter Weir, 1975, The Criterion Collection: Director approved Two-DVD Special Edition Features, 2014, Disc 2, Interview with Peter Weir, 2003, 17:25–17:3.

Polan, Dana. *Jane Campion*. London: British Film Institute, 2001.

"Portrait of a Woman." *Mail & Guardian*, March 14, 1997. https://mg.co.za/article/1997-03-14-portrait-of-a-woman/.

Radner, Hilary. "'In Extremis': Jane Campion and the Woman's Film." In *Jane Campion: Cinema, Nation, Identity,* edited by Hilary Radner, Alistair Fox, and Irène Bessière, 3–26. Detroit, MI: Wayne State University Press, 2009.

Ramanathan, Geetha. *Feminist Auteurs: Reading Women's Films*. London: Wallflower, 2006.

Renov, Michael. *The Subject of Documentary*. Minnesota, MN: University of Minnesota Press, 2004.

Rickey, Carrie. "A Director Strikes an Intimate Chord." In *Jane Campion: Interviews*, edited by Virginia Wright Wexman, 50–3. Jackson: University Press of Mississippi, 1999.

Rilke, Rainer Maria. *Vergers*, translation by Marilyn McCabe. http://numerocinqmagazine.com/2010/12/09/from-vergers-three-poems-by-rilke-translated-by-marilyn-mccabe.

Rose, Jaqueline. *Sexuality in the Field of Vision*. London and New York: Verso, 2005 (1986).

Sarris, Andrew. "Notes on the Auteur Theory in 1962." In *Auteurs and Authorship: A Film Reader*, edited by Barry Keith Grant, 35–45. Malden: Blackwell, 2008.

Silverman, Kaja. *The Acoustic Mirror. The Female Voice in Psychoanalysis and Cinema*. Bloomington, IN and Indianapolis, IN: Indiana University Press, 1988.

Stableford, Brian. *Introduction to Marguerite, Victor, The Bacheloress*. Encino, CA: A Black Coat Press Book, 2015.

Stiles, Mark. "Jane Campion." In *Jane Campion: Interviews*, edited by Virginia Wright Wexman, 3–8. Jackson: University Press of Mississippi, 1999.

Sweetie. The Criterion Collection, 1989, Director's Commentary.

Tatar, Maria. *The Heroine with 1,001 Faces*. New York: Norton, 2021.

The Piano, a film by Jane Campion, The Criterion Collection: Director approved 4K UHD + BluRay Special Edition Features, 2022, Audio Commentary Featuring a Conversation between Campion and Chapman, 37: 12–38:45.

Thornham, Sue. "Starting to Feel Like a Chick." *Feminist Media Studies* 7, no. 1 (2007): 33–46.

Tulich, Katherine. "Jane's Film Career Takes Wing." In *Jane Campion: Interviews*, edited by Virginia Wright Wexman, 71–3. Jackson: University Press of Mississippi, 1999.

Urban, Andrew L. "Hallucination F/X." Interview with Holy Smoke's Digital Effects Supervisor, in Urban Cinefile.

Urban, Andrew L. "The Contradictions of Jane Campion, Cannes Winner." In *Jane Campion: Interviews*, edited by Virginia Wright Wexman, 14–15. Jackson: University Press of Mississippi, 1999.

Uytdewilligen, Ryan. "What is Auteur Theory in Filmmaking?" *InFocus Film School*, November 5, 2019. https://infocusfilmschool.com/auteur-theory-director-filmmakers.

Vattimo, Gianni, Santiago Zabala, and Yaakov Mascetti. "'Weak Thought' and the Reduction of Violence: A Dialogue with Gianni Vattimo." *Common Knowledge* 8, no. 3 (Fall, 2002): 452–63.

Verhoeven, Deb. *Jane Campion*. New York: Routledge, 2005.

Wegenstein, Bernadette, *The Cosmetic Gaze: Body Modification and the Construction of Beauty*,164–74. Cambridge, MA: The MIT Press, 2012.

Wegenstein, Bernadette, dir. *The Conductor*. Waystone Productions, 2021.

Wegenstein, Bernadette and Lauren Mushro, eds. *Radical Equalities and Global Feminist Filmmaking*. Wilmington, DE and Malaga, Spain: Vernon Press, 2022.

White, Patricia. *Women's Cinema, World Cinema: Projecting Contemporary Feminisms*. Durham, NC: Duke University Press, 2015.

White, Patricia. "Women Auteurs, Western Promises." *Film Quarterly* 75, no. 4 (2022): 23–33.

Williams, Sue. "A Light on the Dark Secrets of Depression." In *Jane Campion: Interviews*, edited by Virginia Wright Wexman, 175–6. Jackson: University Press of Mississippi, 1999.

Williamson, Kristen. "The New Filmmakers." In *Jane Campion: Interviews*, edited by Virginia Wright Wexman, 9–10. Jackson: University Press of Mississippi, 1999.

Wittig, Monique. "One Is Not Born a Woman, 1981." In *The Essential Feminist Reader*, edited by Estelle B. Freedman, 359–66. New York: The Modern Library, 2007.

Yuzwalk, Donna. "The Sweet Smell of Success." In *Jane Campion Interviews*, edited by Wright Wexman, 54. Jackson: University Press of Mississippi, 1999.

INDEX